The Shorter Version

By Kathryn Neff Perry

The Shorter Version
© 2007 By Kathryn Neff Perry

Printed On Demand 2007

All rights reserved. No part of this publication may be reproduced, stored in a retrieval system, or transmitted in any form or by any means—for example, electronic, photocopy, and recording— without the prior written permission of the publisher. The only exception is brief quotations in printed reviews.

Trade Paper
ISBN 978-1-60416-098-7

Printed 2007
Williams Printing Company
242 University Drive
Prestonsburg, KY 41653-0276
1-800-765-2464
Information 606-886-7224
Fax 606-886-8222
rpublisher@aol.com
www.reformationpublishers.com

Printed and bound in the United States of America

[THE SHORTER VERSION] By Kathy Perry

This book is dedicated to my Mother. Without her, it would not be possible. These articles were originally published in the Morrow County Sentinel from 1984 to 1989. When I first wrote all these articles I did not save the "master copies." My Father asked me to help him go through her things after she passed away. I was very surprised to find my Mother had cut out each of my articles and stored them in a very safe place, an old shoe box. She dated each of them. I'm not sure if she cut them out as "proof" at a later date, or if she loved me and just wanted to remember how funny she always thought I was.

"The Lord Bless and Keep you.
May the Lord make His face to shine
upon you, may the Lord turn His
face toward you and grant you peace"
Numbers 6:24-27.
Rest in peace Mother.
Bertha May Neff
May 20, 1921 to September 13, 2005

[THE SHORTER VERSION] *By Kathy Perry*

THE NATURAL

Why is it that now it takes a lot longer to attain that natural look of youth. I used to shower, run a big-toothed comb through my long silky hair, and pull on my jeans and t-shirt.

Now, I drag myself out of bed in the morning, put the dog out and plug in the teapot before I ever look in the mirror.

I amble into the bathroom to plug in the hot curlers and the curling iron before I step into the shower. I lather my body with a creamy soap which is supposed to eliminate dry flaky skin. The dandruff shampoo helps tame my gray hair while the cream rinse prevents fly away.

When I climb out of the shower I begin to peel off the green mud pack on my face.

I start with a freshener and then a toner and then comes the foundation, blush eye shadow and lip gloss.

It takes an hour now to dry my hair and curl it.

After I have rubbed lotion on my feet and legs, I lay across the bed to zip my jeans.

I pull on my sweater and yell at my son to hurry up, because I'm ready to leave.

"Hey Jason," I shouted just the other day. "It took me 20 minutes to be this beautiful."

He laughed and replied dryly, "You better take another 20 minutes, Mom."

[THE SHORTER VERSION] *By Kathy Perry*

THE INSTRUCTIONS SAY

My husband came home from work yesterday to find me sitting in the middle of the living room floor. The sweeper was in a million pieces. There was dirt everywhere, including on the end of my nose.

My hair had been neatly tied up on top of my head, but now looked like I'd been caught up in a tornado.

"What are you doing?" he quizzed.

I thought it was obvious.

"I'm trying to repair the sweeper." Was my sarcastic reply.

"It started blowing little dirt balls everywhere, so I thought I would take it apart to see what the problem was."

"Did you find the problem?" He tipped his head and looked me in the eyes.

"Yes, of course," I shouted, "I'm just having a little trouble getting this thing back together."

I knew what he was thinking. He always yells at me for not reading instructions. I usually jump in and if things don't go well, then I dig out the instructions.

Last summer the lawn mower blade needed adjusting. I turned it up on the end and saw two bolts I thought were probably the right ones. That day I had just gotten everything back together when he pulled in the driveway. I stuck the instructions back on the top shelf before he came in the garage.

On the day I put the bookshelf together, I only had two pieces left over.

Right after we bought a camera, the pictures weren't coming out. He asked me, after the second roll of ruined film, if I had read the instructions. I told him the instructions were in Japanese.

Last week Jason was outside trying to launch his rocket. He came in and sat on the sofa looking forlorn.

"Could someone help me launch my rocket?"

"What seems to be the problem" my husband asked.

THE SHORTER VERSION
By Kathy Perry

"I don't know, it just won't take off."
"What did the instructions say?" my husband inquired.
"I don't know, I didn't read them"
My husband glared at me, "I wonder where he gets that?"
"I don't know, he didn't come with instructions."

[THE SHORTER VERSION]   *By Kathy Perry*

DOUBLE IMAGE

The other day when I looked in the mirror, I thought I was seeing double.
You know, two chins, an extra roll around the middle and lots of padding behind me.
I thought what better time than today to start exercising.
Several of my girlfriends have been running and suggested I give it a try.
One of my friends runs over five miles everyday with her husband.
I thought, if Dianne can do it, so can I.
I dressed in blue jeans and an old sweatshirt. I dug my tennis shoes out of the back of the closet. Julie's first reaction was hysteria. When she realized I was serious she begged me not to do it.
"You'll kill yourself, Mom. You are out of shape and you are too old."
I retorted, "Just because I'm old doesn't mean I'm out of shape"
I thought, who does she think she is.
I marched outside confident I could run at least a mile, just because I wanted to.
I tried to pace myself slowly at first, since it was my first day in "training."

I noticed several dogs along the road and some children playing.
I reached a landmark that I felt must have been at least a mile from my house. I slowed down and looked around. When I looked back, completely winded, I could still see my house. I knew I was only about five hundred feet. I was certain I'd already run several miles.

[THE SHORTER VERSION]   *By Kathy Perry*

Every fiber in my body ached. I could hardly breathe as I stumbled back down the road to my house.

I slowly climbed the steps into the house, trying to steady myself as I went.

Julie jumped off the couch when she saw me drag myself into the dining room.

"Mom" she shouted," you look awful. Your lips are blue. Your face is red. I knew it Mom, you're probably having a heart attack right this minute."

I held my stomach as I pushed past her, still unable to speak.

I wanted to tell her my hair hurt too, but I couldn't talk.

I sat on the bedroom floor to remove my shoes and immediately my toes curled.

The muscles in my legs were having spasms.

I thought I would have to crawl to the shower in the bathroom.

After a while I started feeling human again, so I called one of my friends who runs all the time. I wanted to share my horrible story with her.

She said, "Did you do stretching exercises before and after you ran?"

"Stretching exercises? Nobody mentioned stretching exercises."

"Well, she said calmly, tomorrow will be a lot easier."

Tomorrow, she must be joking. I headed to the kitchen to make a banana split and work on chin number three.

[THE SHORTER VERSION]   *By Kathy Perry*

SOCK IT TO ME

Last Sunday morning while we were getting ready for church, my husband found one navy blue sock and one brown sock with about a hundred other mismatched socks. He decided Sunday afternoon he would spring clean his drawers.

"Go ahead," I shouted with enthusiasm from the sofa where I was comfortably watching my usual Sunday afternoon movie.

He yelled to all of us. "Now can any of you explain what has happened to my socks?"

"Don't look at me" shouted Jason. "You know I only wear white socks."

"He even wears them to church," retored Julie. She shrugged her shoulders and looked at us like we were all crazy.

Amy looked at her little feet like 'I'm not the guilty one'.

"What I don't understand," he continued, "is why don't I have the mate to these socks?"

He held several stray socks in the air.

"I never wear one blue sock with a black, or a black with a brown one."

"Don't look at me." I shouted.

Then he started on Simon. My precious, little, innocent dachshund.

"How dare you accuse my little lamb!"

He ran to me knowing I would protect him.

"I know that little mutt of yours is dragging my socks somewhere" he yelled.

"If you didn't leave them on the floor," I protested.

I turned around to see Simon proudly dragging one sock through the living room.

"There, I told you!" he pointed indignantly. "I told you he's the one."

I decided I'd had enough cleaning and walked back to the sofa to finish my nap.

My husband came in and sat at the end of the sofa.

THE SHORTER VERSION
By Kathy Perry

"Here," he patted his leg, "put your feet up here, I'll rub them for you."

I wish I had my camera to capture the look on his face when he looked at my feet. I was wearing one of his blue and one of his brown socks.

[THE SHORTER VERSION] *By Kathy Perry*

WATERBED MANIA

I remember when we first bought our waterbed. The salesman gave me all the positive arguments about why everyone in the world should own a waterbed. Especially someone with back problems.

The longer he talked the more convinced I was, but being "Scotch" I had to look around and think it over a few days before I finally went back to buy the bed.

Now after almost three years of ownership, I'm wondering about all the things he didn't stress.

I was a little concerned about making the bed, so that when I climbed in, the sheets wouldn't pull off the corners. No problem,- Supersalesman said-you just push here, here, here and here, indicating the four corners. Well, that's fine if you are Alex Karras! Super salesman also neglected to mention the fact that once the bed is in place, it is permanent.

One night I woke up about 3:00 a.m. feeling like a popcicle. Our room isn't heated and that cold winter night neither was the water in the bed. We had to drain all 200 gallons through a garden hose out the bedroom window just to remove the heater which is placed under the mattress. It took three more days to fill the mattress and reheat the water before we could sleep on the bed again.

Every six months or so it's necessary to pour a little bottle of treatment solution in the water. So after I had the plug out, ready to dump in the bottle of solution, my sweet little puppy dog Simon jumped on the bed.

I have finally learned after all this time, not to plan anything else on the day I want to change the sheets. The kids just stand back and watch me carefully put the sheets on, only to have each corner slowly slip back off as soon as I turn my back.

[THE SHORTER VERSION]   By Kathy Perry

I'M COMING HOME AGAIN

I'd like to know if there's an unwritten law somewhere that states how many times your kids move out and then back in.

The wonderful part is that each time they move out, they take more of their stuff with them. The bad part is that when they move back in, they have more stuff.

When they moved out they didn't have a washer, dryer, stove or refrigerator, they didn't need one.

My daughter informed me just the other day that she didn't want me to use her towels because "they are too nice." I was also instructed not to use her iron, ironing board or the pots and pans that were sitting on my kitchen counter.

My husband warned me about two weeks ago. "It's all your fault," he stated. "Remember when you decided about three months ago to convert her room into an office for yourself. You thought that was wonderful. You finally had a place to call your own."

I could close the door, and sit at my computer and write my little heart out, or I could study, away from all the noise downstairs.

My husband declared last week was the clincher, when I bought a plant and then I dragged him upstairs. "Look," I shouted, don't you just love my new office?"

The next day my daughter called to see if she could move back to "her old room."

[THE SHORTER VERSION] *By Kathy Perry*

MY FIRST LOVE

Remember your first love?
I hadn't seen Larry for 22 years until the other night.
I recognized him right away. While driving there I wondered if he would be fat, or bald, or even worse, hard of hearing, since it had been so long. But he looked wonderful.
Seeing him made me feel 15 again. I remembered the first time I saw him. I was 15 and he was home for summer break from Ohio State. He was in my Sunday school class. When I first noticed him he was staring at me too. The next time he looked my way I could feel my face turn crimson. It was another week before he finally asked me out. I remember trying to act like I didn't realize he was walking towards me. He probably thought I was in complete control because I hardly moved. Actually I was trying to keep from fainting. I watched his lips move when he asked me for my first date. I couldn't hear what he was saying because my ears were pounding. Then in my most grown up voice I whispered, "I'll have to ask my Mother."
The next few hours were an eternity until my Mother finally agreed to let me go.
The next week was two years long. I picked out 50 different outfits and tried each of them on 20 times.
I talked to my girlfriends who had already had "dates" and asked them what to do about sweaty palms. I bought several different shades of lipstick and new perfume. I was terrified my deodorant would fail half way through the evening.
One of my girlfriends said, "You know Katt, he may try to kiss you good night."
I could feel my face turn red again-just the thought. He wouldn't do that it's our first date! Then he would find out--- I've never been kissed before. Well, guess what!?

[THE SHORTER VERSION]   *By Kathy Perry*

GREEN BEANS VS KIDS

I wish kids were as easy to "grow" as green beans. For instance, if you just dump a little fertilizer on green beans and apply some water once in a while, pull out a few weeds, presto, you have green beans.

Unlike kids who wake up hungry, ravenous would be a better word. They eat one continuous meal, from the time they get up until the time they go to sleep. Sometimes I think my son eats in his sleep, because there are usually Twinkie wrappers on his nightstand, next to the empty milk glass.

I wondered why there were only a few glasses in the cabinet.

I found some of our good china in the basement with cat food on them.

Green beans don't tie up the phone line, or receive calls which tie up the line for hours.

You don't have to worry where your green beans are at night, or what they are doing.

Green beans don't talk back to you, and they don't think you are stupid.

Green beans don't use your makeup, your clothes, or your hair dryer, and then leave them wherever they were when they used them.

Green beans don't dirty dishes and their room and then disappear until bedtime.

However green beans don't make cute little birthday cards, or give you kisses right after they eat chocolate chip cookies.

Maybe I'll keep them---the kids.

[THE SHORTER VERSION] *By Kathy Perry*

CHRISTMAS SPIRIT

It is amazing how everyone is suddenly excited by Christmas when it snows and their spirit is somewhat "dampened" by rain.
I hate those people who finish all their Christmas shopping by October. They are just too organized. They are the careful planners who also have their house decorated inside and out by December 1$^{st.}$
They take their time baking cookies and making candy.
They take the time to make Christmas decorations for the tree.
Their house usually looks like a page from "Country Living."
About this time of the year my house looks like a page from "Popular Mechanics."
I have 14 projects started and three of them are spread out on the dining room table.
Every year I promise myself I will start earlier on everything. I like to make Christmas presents and next year I will start in July. In fact that may just be one of my New Year resolutions.
Things were very different for my kids than they were for me when I was a kid.
Even the traditional songs I used to sing, like Silent Night or Jingle Bells or Sleigh Ride.
My kids walk through the house singing "Grandma got run over by a Reindeer."
My, times have changed.

[THE SHORTER VERSION] By Kathy Perry

TRIBAL WARNINGS

I remember when my kids were little and I had to get up in the middle of the night. I'd try to change them with one eye open, hoping I didn't stab them with the safety pin. That was before the days of disposable diapers with self-fastening tabs.

I would walk the floor or try to sing or anything just to get the kid back to sleep, all the while wishing my life would return to normal. Or at least my sleep. You know, like going to bed when I felt like it and sleeping all night. Little did I know that I would never see "normal" again.

When they were little, I could put them in bed for a nap and I usually took one too.

Now, when I try to take a nap, it sounds like drums from a distant tribe, trying to warn someone. The tribal sounds come from their rooms, or from their cars, the warnings can be heard from roughly two miles away.

When I needed to sew, or iron, I could stick them in a playpen to keep them entertained.

Now it costs anywhere from $20 to $40 to entertain them. And that doesn't include the cost of feeding them.

I used to be able to make faces at them to make them laugh. Now all I have to do is say, "I thought you were going to do the dishes?"

I remember being disgusted when my son spit peas on me. He used to dump everything on the floor. He loved to throw mashed potatoes against the wall.

It used to be quite an ordeal moving his high chair to the middle of the room and only giving him one thing at a time.

My life hasn't really changed a whole lot over the past 20 years. I still wake up in the middle of the night and check to make sure they are safely in their bed. I don't have to change diapers or feed them in the middle of the night.

[THE SHORTER VERSION] *By Kathy Perry*

I think some of the tribal drums might have impaired their hearing though, because just this morning I shouted, "Who wants to help me work in the garden?" and nobody heard me.

[THE SHORTER VERSION] *By Kathy Perry*

STUPID QUESTIONS

Why is it that my kids only have one speed when they are doing something for me, like the dishes. They wash two cups, one fork and maybe a dinner plate, and the rest of the dishes "have to soak."

I remember once I asked one of them to run the sweeper. I think they either said, "I just ran it for you two weeks ago, or "I'll do it after while."

I think more than anything, I love the "pet story."

"Please Mom, please. It always starts out. "Everybody I know has a cat. It isn't fair that we can't have one. Angela's Mom is letting her get one of the kittens too."

"Besides, I promise I'll take care of her. I'll feed her everyday and I'll clean the litter box."

Well, after two weeks of arguing and feeling guilty because I'm not like everybody else's mom, I finally did give in.

The day she brought the cat home was a ritual that should have had media coverage.

She carried in cat litter, a litter box, a color coordinated "little scooper" and 17 "educational toys" for the little cat. Who could also by the way catch mice.

Julie bought three different kinds of gourmet cat food, because she didn't know what kind "kitty" would like.

Now just three months later, the cat has of course run out of the cat food my daughter bought. Her litter box "runneth over" and as far as the mice go, she did catch one. She brought it to me. She sat down in front of me, turned the mouse loose, only to catch it again and of course turn it loose again.

I asked Julie a stupid question just the other day. I asked her if she knew how many times the cat used the litter box in three months.

She gave me a disgusted look (she was doing her nails), but she assured me she would "get to it tomorrow."

[THE SHORTER VERSION] *By Kathy Perry*

ENERGY CRUNCH HITS HOME

Last week I realized that everything was getting out of hand. The grocery bills are skyrocketing. The utilities are still too high. We've been spending too much on gasoline.

As I sat at the dining room table drinking my Chai tea, I decided my next project would be to cut the budget. Large corporations do it all the time.

From now on everyone will have to be energy conscious.

I decided to sit down with each family member and discuss my new plan.

I started with Jason. I tried to explain that it isn't necessary to pre-heat his soldering iron for an hour. It's also not necessary to lie on his bed with headphones in listening to the stereo while he's watching his favorite tv show without the sound.

Julie was next on the list. "Why do you need all these curling irons?" Do they really need to be plugged in all day? You know, we're not running a beauty shop."

"Mom, just trust me. I do need four curling irons. Each one of them does a different part of my hair."

"Why do you need hot curlers, too?"

"They are for the back of my hair."

As I walked around her room with my clipboard in hand, I noticed the iron was also plugged in.

"How long has the iron been on?"

"Gosh, Mom, I don't know. I ironed my blouse this morning."

"It's 6:00 at night," I protested.

I was beginning to realize why our electric bill is so high.

Amy's reasoning for leaving the light on all night was because she saw "something on the wall."

"Why can't you turn the light on to make sure it's just a shadow, then turn it off and go back to sleep?"

"Because Mom, something might come out of my closet."

By the time my husband got home I was feeling pretty defeated.

[THE SHORTER VERSION] By Kathy Perry

"You know, I've been talking to the kids this afternoon about being more energy conscious, but they don't understand."
He walked over and put his arms around me.
"It'll be okay." Then he sat in his chair to read the paper.
"By the way," I turned to him. "We got the phone bill today. We've got to cut down on the long distance calls."
He lowered the paper and waited.
"How many calls did we have?"
"There were four."
"Well, how much were they?"
"Seventy cents."

[THE SHORTER VERSION] *By Kathy Perry*

CONVERSATIONS IN THE DARK

The only conversations I ever have with my children are short ones.
For instance, they ask, "Mom, are my jeans clean? What do we have to eat? Who used all the hot water?" I haven't figured out why they will spend $40 or $50 on a pair of designer jeans for a boyfriend or girlfriend they were never going to speak to again, and buy Mom a coffee mug with one "M" missing from "MOM."
They offer to wash their boyfriend's car, or clean his apartment, but they're too busy to wash the dishes or clean their own room.
When it's time to cut the grass or take out the trash, my son becomes comatose.
I usually try to "catch up" on the weekends, since I'm still working full time and driving to Columbus two nights a week.
On the weekend when I'm in the middle of laundry, cleaning the house or trying to cut the grass, one of them usually says, "I'm bored, Mom."
Just the other day my son was stretched out on the sofa watching a movie., There were banana peels everywhere.
I shouted, "Pick up those banana peels!"
He very calmly replied, "I did, I put them there."

[THE SHORTER VERSION] By Kathy Perry

HOW LONG HAS IT BEEN

I think most moms, at some time during their career in motherhood, wonder what kind of person their children will marry.
I think for the last 16 years my son has been giving me "clues." For instance, just the other evening, I know my future daughter-in-law will have a good sense of humor. I came home from work, after picking up Amy from the babysitters, washed two loads of laundry, cooked dinner, washed the dishes, studied for an hour and finally sat down at 10:30 p.m. My son said, "You know what Mom, some tapioca pudding sure would taste good to me."
To which I replied, "There is an easy recipe on the back of the box. I'll be glad to help you, if you have trouble with the big words, like milk or sugar."
My future daughter-in-law will have to know how to skin and cook a ground hog, and probably like to eat it too, because he won't unless she can disguise it in a taco shell.
She will have to be able to cook a seven-course meal over an open fire, because he wants to live off the land."
She will probably speak French fluently because every year when he goes hunting or fishing in Canada, she'll be able to ask, "Where's the nearest McDonalds'?
Just the other day he told me he thought he would wash all his bedding, the sheets, blankets, and bed spread.
He yelled at me, "Don't act like it's such a big deal Mom."
I smiled at him, "How long has it been since you've washed your own bedding?"
He gave me a nasty look. "I don't know Mom, how long have we lived here?"

[THE SHORTER VERSION] *By Kathy Perry*

THIS DIET IS FOR ME

My husband said just the other day that he was really proud of me because of my diet.

He said, "You know, you are the only person I know who can be on a diet and eat strawberry shortcake with whipped cream, Ho Ho's, cookies, Drumsticks, bread sticks with cheese sauce, and banana splits."

I replied, "Well, look at it this way. When I tell you every year that I "need" a new wardrobe, I really do "need" one. (A few sizes larger).

I used to wear jeans, but now I buy stretch pants-the ones with the elastic waistbands.

My bathing suit this summer looks similar to the ones on the maternity rack.

I thought I'd tell people I started drinking Weight On, and it worked.

People always used to ask me how I stayed so thin---I'm glad I don't have to be bothered with that question anymore.

If you ask me, there are several advantages to being fat. You don't have to worry about a diet anymore.

I hate all that diet stuff—all those diet colas and salad. I think eventually that stuff will kill you.

As far as I am concerned homemade ice cream with chocolate, nuts and whipped cream is the only diet for me.

[THE SHORTER VERSION] By Kathy Perry

GOING HOME

I asked my Mother the other day if I could stay all night, even though our houses are only minutes apart.
She said, "It's not the same."
I promised not to leave toothpaste in the sink, or a half full glass of milk in the family room. I told her I would not leave my dirty underwear under my bed.
"I promise, Mom, I won't forget to unplug the iron."
I'll even unload the dishwasher. I could envision stretching out on my bed with a plate of brownies sitting on the nightstand beside a tall glass of cold milk. The Beach Boys were singing "Surfer Girl," and my girlfriends were coming over later for pizza and Pepsi to watch a movie.
I thought I could hear Mom yell, "Don't forget to put your clothes away, I spent the entire day doing your laundry."
I felt a small hand on my shoulder.
It was Amy.
"Mom, are you going to sleep all day? I'm hungry."

[THE SHORTER VERSION] *By Kathy Perry*

CONFESSIONS

I had such a busy week. We've been so busy at work, so I've had to work everyday. No more part time. This was also finals week, which meant there were several nights I was up burning the proverbial midnight oil. Needless to say I was pretty tired.

I always look forward to being able to sleep until at least 9:00 on Saturday morning, but unfortunately Saturday I have a convention and must be in Columbus by 7:30 a.m. Simon and I were all snuggled up together on the sofa ready for a nap when my husband sat down beside us.

"Is there anything I can do for you," he asked.

"Well, actually, do you think you could write my article this week? I am so tired, I can't think."

He laughed. "Sure, I'll just start out like this."

"This is Kathy's husband, I'm writing her article this week because she's asleep."

"No, I didn't cut down all the trees, I don't care how fat she gets, I won't divorce her and no I don't want an indoor pool."

[THE SHORTER VERSION] *By Kathy Perry*

ON HIS OWN

My husband is afraid of large appliances. You know, like stoves, refrigerators, washers or dryers.
I'm speculating that he had a traumatic experience as a child.
He will often come in the kitchen and lift the lid. I don't know why, because he turns to me and says, "What's for dinner?"
On rare occasions when I'm not home and I ask him to cook lunch or dinner, the kids usually offer to take him out to eat.
Once I asked him to make Jello. Now you have to remember this man is not a moron, but we had to cut the Jello with a steak knife. He's tried his hand at oatmeal a time or two, but it turns out like little hushpuppies or little dough balls.
One time when I was recovering from an accident he, was hungry for homemade bread. I told him to call his mother.
This same man is a whiz if you put an apron on him, stick a fork in his hand, and shove him outside. He can grill anything, once he gets the grill lit---well that's another column!

[THE SHORTER VERSION] By Kathy Perry

IT TAKES THE LUMPS OUT

If it comes in a box, or it's frozen with microwave instructions, my daughter can whip up a nine-course meal.
Hand her a cookbook and she panics.
It's not a matter of intelligence or ability, because she is a very capable girl.
My husband is the same way. If I'm not home he would rather make a peanut butter sandwich than warm something in the microwave.
My son likes to cook pancakes. I buy the pre-mixed kind, all he has to do is add water-then throw them in the skillet.
Each of them excels at something, or so they claim. My daughter bakes chocolate chip cookies, my son, pancakes and my husband tries to make Jello.
Amy and I just eat out.
The other day some ice got stuck in the blender and I couldn't turn if off fast enough to "save" it.
A blender is a must in my kitchen because it takes out the lumps.
As we were waiting in line to pay for our new blender, Amy turned to me and said, I think in her loudest voice, "I'm so glad you're buying another blender, Mom, now you can make gravy again."

[THE SHORTER VERSION] By Kathy Perry

NO MORE NAPS

I think one of the big mistakes in my life is trying to take a nap. I remember when my children were younger, I had been awakened during the night several times, how I couldn't wait until the afternoon when they were both asleep so I could rest too. I remember one of them would hardly ever cooperate. If they did fall asleep at the same time, I would sleep with one eye open.

One such afternoon when they were both pretty young comes to mind. Those were the days when they liked each other. They wanted to take a nap together. I didn't know any better then.

I also took a nap. What woke me was the silence. I knew by my watch too much time had passed. As I neared my daughter's room, I could hear muffled giggles. I peeked in the door, only to find they were having a great time. They had taken the blankets, sheets and mattress pad off her bed and had drawn an entire village of stick people on her mattress.

Another day during a short nap, my son, who was probably about two at the time, was cleaning the aquarium with a toilet bowl brush. That time my daughter's screams woke me, because several of her beloved fish were in the middle of the kitchen floor. Not only was he "cleaning" the aquarium, he was also taking the fish out, but couldn't hold on to them.

My husband, you remember the "Les Nesman" of my life, has convinced me to give up naps forever. Yesterday he was outside burning trash when the wind shifted. It wasn't funny yesterday, but today I'm hysterical. It singed most of the hair on the right side of his face, neck and arms. Next time you see him, ask him to lift his right arm.

[THE SHORTER VERSION] *By Kathy Perry*

OLE' BLUE

Now that summer is finally here, I think it's too late for that last minute crash diet.

Julie has been telling me for six months I should diet.

Everyone at work drinks diet this and diet that. They eat salad with lo-cal dressing, and cottage cheese with tomatoes. They talk about starving on yogurt and diet 7 UP.

It doesn't usually bother me when they talk about a size 5 or 7. I used to wear a 5 when I was about 10 years old.

Half the girls at the lunch table also work out at the spa three days a week.

Julie wanted to go swimming the other day, so I decided to dig out my old faithful swimsuit. I've had it for years. It's almost become a part of me. Actually I didn't think it looked too bad. It's a pretty robin's egg blue with big white flowers.

Julie remarked she wouldn't be caught dead with me wearing that suit.

"Not another year, Mom. You have to get a new one. I know you hate to spend the money," she continued, "and another thing, I told you six months ago you should be dieting. Look at all those little fat rolls." I didn't think they looked so bad. Maybe I should give up 'old blue' and buy one of those newer suits that have a more slimming effect. The fact is, I really do hate to give up 'old blue' until the knees wear out.

[THE SHORTER VERSION] *By Kathy Perry*

DAD DOESN'T LISTEN TO ANYBODY

Amy complains sometimes because her Dad doesn't listen to her. I told her not to feel bad because he doesn't listen to me either.

At breakfast he's usually behind the sports page of the morning paper.

The only time he looks up or discusses anything with us is if we know (or care about) the latest scores.

When he comes home at night, tired from a long day, he just wants to sit and watch tv.

If you can get his attention, sometimes he'll nod.

During a commercial, he usually asks one of us to stick a cup of water in the microwave for a cup of coffee.

Now, if a football game happens to be on the tube, it is impossible to get his attention. If the house was on fire, it would burn down around him. If we had company, they better like football too.

The other day poor Amy was pretty upset. She had tried several times to get her father's attention. She finally came over and sat down beside me.

I patted her hand and said, "Amy, you just don't know how to talk to him, let me share my secret. First, I go in my bedroom and put on shoulder pads, knee pads, a football helmet, and then I run into the family room and toss a football to him----It works every time.

[THE SHORTER VERSION] *By Kathy Perry*

GLAD I'M A GIRL

I remember a million years ago, when I was a little girl and I used to count the days, minutes and hours until summer vacation.

I thought it was terrible that I had to get up at 6:00 a.m., ride a bus for an hour, sit in classrooms all day, then ride the dumb bus home again.

I always thought I was so lucky to be a girl because girls grow up to be moms, who don't have to work as hard as dads do.

I always thought my adult life would be a piece of cake. Nothing compared to the way it was when I was 10.

I didn't like having someone tell me when to go to bed, or when to get up. Someone else picked out my clothes. I didn't have the opportunity to choose what I would be eating for dinner, because Mom cooked it.

Today is a different story.

I would love to have a bus stop out front to pick me up, no charge, and take me to work. I would not have to buy gas, insurance, or find a parking spot. I also wouldn't have a car payment.

Wouldn't it be nice if someone would take me shopping for "school clothes." I wouldn't care if they picked them out, as long as they paid for them.

How nice it would be to sit down at the table to eat food that someone else had prepared. After they did the grocery shopping. And then they cleaned the kitchen and did the dishes while I took a little nap.

Oh yes, and a three month paid vacation every summer would be nice too.

Piece of cake.

That's what I thought this afternoon on my way home from work, because before I left this morning, I washed two loads of clothes, put the dishes away, ran the sweeper. I drove to work and after eight hours came back home. After I cooked dinner, I

[THE SHORTER VERSION] By Kathy Perry

drove to Columbus to school. I didn't have time to eat. I drove back home after class and washed the dishes from dinner and folded one last load of clothes so everyone would have clean towels in the morning.

Finally at 12:30 a.m. I plopped in a comfortable chair, kicked off my shoes, propped my feet up as I drank my favorite, Suisse Mocha.

I sighed to myself, yes, I'm sure glad I'm a girl.

[THE SHORTER VERSION] *By Kathy Perry*

THE JOYS OF AMERICA

Last night I watched a movie where the star got hit in the head and she couldn't remember who she was.

I used to read about people who suffered from amnesia and felt sorry for them. That was before I was the mother of teenagers. Now I think one of the most wonderful gifts would be to suffer from amnesia once in a while.

Like maybe on Friday night after I drop my son off at the Purple Indian. I'd regain my memory on Tuesday.

Sometimes I think my own children suffer from amnesia. When I ask my son to burn the trash, he says he will in a minute, usually after he does his homework.

When I ask them to clean their rooms they usually say they'll do it later, after a short nap-because they are too tired from their long day at school.

I probably shouldn't complain, because my children are pretty talented.

Years ago I found a poem my son dedicated to his sister, "Boys go to Mars to get more candy bars-Girls go to Jupiter to get more stupider."

Just as recently as a few weeks ago, my little Amy left a legacy of her own. She brought home a paper from the PTO Carnival and on that paper she was supposed to fill in her name and address and any special talent she might possess. Imagine my surprise when she wrote "break dancing."

[THE SHORTER VERSION] *By Kathy Perry*

MY HOME TOWN

I was reading an article that really caught my eye the other day. It was a comparison of living expenses through the United States.
So I tried to gather as much of the information as I could and this is how I plan to live for the next few months, just to see how much money I can save.
I'm going to rent an apartment in Jonesboro, AK.
I'll be buying aspirin in Youngstown. For entertainment, I'll be bowling in New York City and I'll buy my son's underwear in Jonesboro. I'll buy cheeseburgers in Indianapolis, IN.
I'll buy Pepsi in San Diego, CA, and coffee in Youngstown, the same time I buy aspirin.
When I have my teeth cleaned it will be right after I eat cheeseburgers in Indianapolis. I'll be dropping my husband's suit to be cleaned in Chattanooga, TN.
I'll be driving to Casper WY to buy gasoline and of course I'll be pumping it myself. If I cook again and need ground beef, I'll buy it the same time I pick up the coffee and aspirin in Youngstown.
When I get my hair done I have two choices, I can go to Youngstown when I buy coffee, aspirin and ground beef, or Jonesboro where my apartment and son's underwear are.
If I have to stay in the hospital it's back to Jonesboro.
If I need Kleenex or milk, Youngstown's the winner.
I'm building a new house in Rapid City, SD, where I will also have my washer repaired.
And if I'm not too tired after saving all that money, I'll go to a movie in Mt. Gilead, Ohio.

[THE SHORTER VERSION]   *By Kathy Perry*

A WEEK OFF

I don't remember how it came about. I believe it was strictly by accident.
Everybody in my family left, and I was alone for a week.

Amy was the only one who realized that I would be alone.
The week before she left she kept asking me if I would be homesick. I told her I would try to stick it out.
"I know it will be tough, Amy, but I think I can do it."
Somehow I made it through the week. Since my children were born, I think that was the first time I was alone for that length of time.
It was awful!
I came home from work every night to find the house just the way I left it. There were no dirty dishes in the sink, on the counter, or on the coffee table.
There wasn't enough laundry for a full load.
I was able to eat Cream of Wheat every morning with milk on it. I always check before I go to bed to see if there is milk, and in the morning I cook Cream of Wheat, but the milk disappears sometime during the night.
I bought a box of Twinkies, and ate one every night before I went to bed.
I only ran the sweeper once because no one was there to track anything through the house.
I feel stronger now. It was a tough week, but I survived!

[THE SHORTER VERSION] By Kathy Perry

MOTHERHOOD-WHAT FUN

I think the nicest part of motherhood is the mess they leave behind, just to remind you that you have children.

I came home from work the other day to learn I definitely have children. From the way my house looked, I would have guessed about 23 of them.

I had several bags of groceries, but nowhere to sit them. From the looks of things, my children had a pretty nice dinner. Of course they saved some for me!

The clothes were still on the couch where I threw them that morning, not having time before I left for work to fold them. Someone sat on them because they were wrinkled and flat.

There were several dirty cups sitting on the coffee table.

My daughter was resting comfortably in my bed, because she had a bad day.

My son, Trapper John, was outside tending to a huge bonfire in the middle of the back yard. I yelled, trying to understand why he built a fire in the middle of the yard, using wood for the fireplace that I had to pay for. He had a large pot on the tripod with his traps in boiling hot water.

"Let me see if I understand," I started, "you made me pay for new traps so you could put them in a big pot of boiling water so they will rust."

He mumbled something, then looked at me like I was brain dead.

When I came back outside, after shoving everything aside and setting the bags of groceries on the counter, I noticed Trapper John had hung all his traps on the light post.

"Why would you do that?" I shouted.

He looked at me with his big brown eyes. "I was just thinking of you Mother, I didn't want you to back over them with your car."

THE SHORTER VERSION By Kathy Perry

OH, JUST THE USUAL DAY

I don't think my children are really very different from anyone else's children and my husband probably isn't either.

Why is it whenever anything happens the children call "The MOM" and not "The DAD?"

Just once, I would love to come home from work, sit down to read the newspaper and casually say, "How was your day dear," and have my husband be able to reply as follows:

"We were so busy at work today. I feel like I've been run over by a train. The kids called me several times. Once to remind me we are out of ketchup. The next time was because Jason forgot to the take the permission slip I signed for the field trip with him, so I had to give permission over the phone to his teacher, while two people were on hold. The third time was to see if I knew anyone who wanted a puppy.

When I pulled in the driveway I saw the kid's cat along the side of the road. So of course I had to tell them about their cat, and then bury it myself.

I came in the house, worked my way into the kitchen by picking up shoes, clothes, cups, plates, coats and books along the way. I discovered the dog had eaten a pair of Reeboks. The son called to say his car died on the way to work and could I call his grandfather to fix it and could I hurry to pick him up and take him to work on time.

Then after I cooked dinner, washed the dishes, washed and dried three loads of laundry, I finally sat down to read the paper.

Or maybe my husband would say, "Oh, just the usual day dear."

[THE SHORTER VERSION] By Kathy Perry

EVEN WHISPERING HURTS

A few weeks ago, I somehow managed to get the worst sore throat I've had for many years. After several days I finally lost my voice. I couldn't talk above a whisper, and even whispering hurt.

It wasn't too bad at work because everyone knew I couldn't talk because my job is talking to the public so I did odd jobs for a week or so until I could talk again.

But at home, the first day my husband came home from work and told me all about his day while I was in the kitchen cooking. He went into the other room to read the paper and after dinner, in fact about two hours after he came home, he came back out in the kitchen while I was cleaning the kitchen and said "are you upset with me, you've hardly said two words since I've been home?"

Amy is so used to hearing me tell her to pick up her shoes. She leaves her shoes in the dining room or living room and every night before she goes to bed I always remind her to pick up her shoes. Since I couldn't talk, she lost one pair of shoes because Buddy loves to chew on them. Every morning I would find Buddy in the dining room chewing on another pair of Amy's shoes. Some mornings I think he had a smile on his face.

The very worst offenders were my two oldest.

My son called to ask permission for something and when I whispered "no" to him, he said "thanks a lot, mom," and hung up.

Julie said a few words before she realized I had no voice.

You don't realize how much you need your voice until you don't have it. I went to the store and in a whisper I tried to tell the clerk what I needed. She leaned close to me and whispered, "what did you say?"

[THE SHORTER VERSION] *By Kathy Perry*

WHAT FUN

I've noticed the older I get, the worse my memory is.

For instance, I remember sitting on the floor in front of my son trying to get him to say "Mama" and "Dada" and "Teddy Bear." I don't remember teaching him to say "Can I borrow your car, "or "I need gas money." I always had to play games with him to get him to eat.

I would pretend the spoon was an airplane and I was coming in for a "landing." That was his clue to open his mouth. One day he was being extremely difficult. He made me run all over the kitchen with that stupid spoon acting like I was an airplane before he would take a bite. It's no wonder I didn't weigh very much back then.

One day my mother was visiting during dinner time. By this time he was a little older and a lot more independent. He was a "big boy," and he wanted to feed himself. Every time I put a plate on his highchair tray he would drop it on the floor and watch the food splatter, then he would laugh and clap his hands.

Things aren't a whole lot different today. He doesn't sit in a high chair, nor does he throw his plate on the floor. He slaps peanut butter on the counter and leaves the bread out. He puts the milk back in the fridge when there is only a tablespoon left. His grandmother thinks I should just dump food on a tray for him the way I used to. Nobody told me it would be this much fun.

[THE SHORTER VERSION] — *By Kathy Perry*

I'VE BEEN REPLACED

I learned last evening that this may be the last time I write for the paper. Yes, that's right, I may have been replaced.

As we were planting trees and weeding the shrubs, Amy advised me that she's going to write a book.

I told her I thought that was wonderful.

I asked her if she had any definite ideas about her first book, and she gave me a few tips on what she planned to write about. Mostly just her life experiences so far. How she's organized her "Fun Club." I suggested she write a "How to" book. It was 7:30 p.m. when she informed me that she would have her first book ready for "press" before bedtime. (8:30 p.m.)

We discussed the fact that sometimes it takes writers a little longer than an hour to write an entire book.

I suggested that maybe she should start out on a smaller scale, like an article.

Then she looked at me with those big green eyes and said, "Yeah Mom, on those nights when you're "too tired to move, I can write an article for you!"

[THE SHORTER VERSION] *By Kathy Perry*

MY DOG BUDDY

My husband always makes fun of me because he says my dogs live better lives than some people.
I think he's crazy. I don't think my dogs live any differently than any other dog.
For instance, Koko has a little sweater, and Buddy has a couple of scarves. He looks really cute in his little red scarf. One day my husband asked why he didn't have sunglasses. I told him they wouldn't stay on his face.
Buddy and Koko are always in the same room I am in. Or, if I'm outside, they always want to be with me. Buddy, the Rottweiller, is too big to sit on my lap, but he always want to be able to see me. Koko, the Daschund, just sits in the chair beside me.
They get the usual treats everyone gives their dog. A dog biscuit or a rawhide treat. Sometimes they each get a little ice cream cone.
They both have their own special brush. Buddy is short-haired and Koko is long-haired.
I think the only thing that might be the least bit unusual is my dogs both like ice water. In the summer when it is really hot, I keep their water dish filled with ice water.
I think what got me in trouble was, the other night I was having a glass of iced tea and when my dogs heard me getting the ice out of the freezer they both started barking, and ran to the kitchen as fast as they could. My husband thought something happened to me and hurried to see what the problem was. When I handed each of my dogs an ice cube and they ran to their favorite spot to eat it, I knew what he was talking about.

[THE SHORTER VERSION] *By Kathy Perry*

LIFE JUST ISN'T FAIR

My girlfriend Ellie called the other day. She was yelling, "If I don't win the lottery pretty soon, I don't know what I'm going to do." Life just isn't fair," she continued.

I realized how unhappy she was and how unhappy she had been, but I wasn't totally convinced that winning the lottery would bring her all the happiness she was looking for.

After we hung up, I thought about her for a long time.

I thought about all the things that make me happy, that have nothing to do with money.

Sometimes my sister, Pat, laughs so hard tears roll down her cheeks-usually at something that's just silly.

A lot of the memories I have are of my grandmother's kitchen. I remember learning to cook and helping her put butter on the top of freshly baked bread.

My mother smiling at me, when I know she's proud I'm her daughter.

When my husband brings me flowers for no reason, or sends me a card because he cares.

When my children ask me to go to a movie or dinner with them and not expect me to pay.

When my dog wags his entire body, just because I walked through the door.

The other day, I cleaned a drawer and found old poems my children had written to me on special occasions telling me they love me.

And most of all, my friends make me happy when they call and say let's have lunch---I miss you.

Someday I hope my friend, Ellie, will realize her family and friends are more important than anything---and if she ever does win the lottery she'll have more friends and family she doesn't know she has.

[THE SHORTER VERSION] *By Kathy Perry*

THE DRIVER

Now that my son has had two lessons (classroom only), he has become an expert on driving. Now when I drive, he grades me. I believe in his own words last night, I actually failed according to him.

I remember numerous occasions when he used to think I was a good driver. He used to say, "someday I hope I drive just like you, mom." I can hardly believe it myself. I think he was six at the time.

So far, I have been the only brave person in our immediate family. My husband let him drive a few times, but the day he drove on the wrong side of the road for about a quarter of a mile because he was making a left-hand turn was the last time they shared that experience.

My father let him drive once. When my father said turn here, my son did, then slammed on the brakes. My father grabbed the dash, then the wheel, and pointed to the curb. My son pulled over and my father drove from there.

Somehow, I wonder how parents and grandparents live through it. My own dear grandmother. I don't remember how I convinced her to ride with me. My father insisted I learn to drive his old pick-up truck with a three-speed transmission. My mother climbed in the front seat with me at the wheel. My grandmother sat in the bed of the truck. Since I was only fifteen at the time I couldn't drive on the road. I drove back through the fields. Grandma held on as best she could.

Maybe that one memory is why my mother is deaf when my kids say, "Hey grandma, you wanna' go for a ride?"

[THE SHORTER VERSION] *By Kathy Perry*

THE BIG 40

Birthdays come and birthdays go. This was my big one---The Big 40.

People are telling me its downhill from now on.

My "friends" at work teased me all day about being "over-the-hill." One of them said she noticed a lot more gray hair. Another mentioned my middle-aged spread.

I still received almost as many cards as candles on my cake, from friends who don't think I'm a gray-haired over the hill lady with a middle aged spread.

By the time I got home that night, I was feeling better and really looking forward to spending the rest of the evening with my family.

We all went out to dinner, and enjoyed each other's company, as usual. I have always appreciated the friendship my sister and I share, that is until this year.

How would you feel on your 40th birthday, if your sister sent you a card like this---on the outside was a picture of "Lucy" (Shultz) on a sofa looking pale and uncomfortable, with sweat on her brow, saying, "Oh, don't worry about me," then on the inside of the card Lucy is sitting up looking recovered, saying "I was just overcome by the heat from the candles on your birthday cake!"

Thanks Sis!

[THE SHORTER VERSION] By Kathy Perry

THE NEXT TEN YEARS

Why is it the only time your kids leave you alone is when you cut the grass, wash the car, fold clothes or wash the dishes?

With the first sign of the sweeper, or laundry detergent they disappear into their rooms for hours.

Now, if I were talking on the phone and not necessarily wanting to include them in the conversation, they remain in the same room with me and try to carry on a conversation that ranges anywhere from what's for dinner to what Vickie Pryor wore to school that day.

If I decide to read a book, they have several projects they forgot to tell me about. Like baking six dozen cookies for school tomorrow, and by the way, it is 8:45 pm the night before and we are out of eggs.

My favorite thing is when I decide to take a nap. About once every six months I lose my mind, and try to take a nap. The second I close my other eye, they declare war, and stake out the demilitarized zone. In my mind, I roll off the sofa and tie each of them to a chair, and wait for the next bomb to drop.

There is usually a loud sound upstairs, which resembles the Ohio State marching band during "Script Ohio."

If the book I'm trying to read right now is correct, then I understand the next 10 years are the ones I'll enjoy the most!

[THE SHORTER VERSION] *By Kathy Perry*

FIT AND TRIM

I think I have always tried to be health conscious, and I've tried to teach my children to eat right, and to get enough sleep and exercise.

So, where did I go wrong? How can they live on the stuff they eat?

My son eats a steady diet of chocolate chip cookies and gallons of milk. He has probably eaten a million boxes of cereal.

Now my daughter, on the other hand, eats macaroni and cheese and tacos.

My husband eats anything on the table. He even chews paper.

Amy and I try to diet. We work out several days a week and try to stay fit.

I nag at my son to get more exercise. I even offered to let him mow the lawn. He said he had to get ready for work. I reminded him it was only Tuesday and he didn't have to work until Friday.

My husband tells me once a week that "tomorrow" he's going to start working out. He usually does wake up and start to do push-ups. He does five and then yells at me to look up the number for the emergency squad. He won't listen when I tell him to start out slow.

Amy and I just recently started a new exercise program, so maybe that's why I've been having such crazy dreams. The other morning as I was waking up, I realized I was having serious chest pains. I could hardly breathe and my entire body felt rigid. While I was still half asleep—I thought this can't be happening to me---then I realized my fat little dog, KOKO had slept on my chest most of the night!

[THE SHORTER VERSION] *By Kathy Perry*

I NEED A BUS BOY

I think one of the differences between an eight year old and an eighteen year old is the eight year old still thinks you know everything and the eighteen year old thinks you shouldn't be trusted with sharp objects.

Since I had a few days off this past week, I had the opportunity to spend time with mothers of teenagers.

I also spent time with mothers of young children.

The contrast between the two is incredible.

When my son was still in the "riding in the grocery cart stage." I used to stroll thru the store casually picking up a few items on my limited budget, trying to keep my eye on my daughter, who was usually a few steps ahead of me trying to buy a few of her own "things." The cereal box with a picture of what toy would be inside.

Imagine my surprise when I reached the check-out and my little cherub in the seat had thrown about $50 worth of "stuff" in my cart. One day I asked Julie to watch him for a second while I ran back to pick up something I had forgotten. When I was on my way back to the cart they were having a tug of war over a bag of chocolate chip cookies. The bag ripped open and there were cookies everywhere. He was stuffing them in his mouth as fast as he could.

If I had known then that those two sweet little children would later be teenagers and turn on me, I would probably have left them at the check-out that day.

I was at Porter's Restaurant the other night and as I was sitting there, the owner yelled, "We need a bus boy out here," and my little cherub came out and cleared off the table.

Now I know what I've been doing wrong. I didn't give him a title. From now on, when I need the trash burned, I'll yell, "I need a trash boy," or the grass cut, I'll yell, "I need a lawn boy." If it works I'll patent it.

[THE SHORTER VERSION] *By Kathy Perry*

IT'S MY FAULT

I decided I had to write an article this week to apologize. Not just to the people in Morrow County, but most of the State of Ohio. Yes, my dear readers, it is my fault, and I'm sorry.

Remember last week when we had 60 and 70 degree weather? I spent an entire day washing sweaters. I even dried them outside. I folded and put them away for the "winter."

I took all our wool slacks and coats to the cleaners—to be cleaned and "sealed" until next winter.

I moved all my warm clothes to the other closet and got all my spring clothes, shoes and light weight jackets, out and ready to wear.

I even bought a new bathing suit (one size larger than last year.)

I'm convinced however, that my last act was the one responsible for the latest dump of white powder upon us. Several weeks ago, I washed and waxed my car (which usually brings on the rain—I call it my modern day rain dance.)

That same afternoon, Amy was riding her bike, and had just changed to shorts.

I decided it was time. I had waited most of the winter to buy a new mailbox, because the snow plow almost always knocks it off, or just the snow from the plow dents it.

After I mounted the new mailbox I made Amy come out and tell me how pretty it was. I told her I was going to plant flowers around it.

Two days later school was cancelled, snow day.

[THE SHORTER VERSION] *By Kathy Perry*

ONE SIZE LARGER

Last week, I think I put "Refrigerator Perry" to shame. If it wasn't nailed down, I ate it. Cookies, pies, cakes and hot fudge sundaes (with whipped cream and nuts).
Some of the girls I work with are having a "weight loss contest." Whoever loses the most weight wins the money.
One of the girls said she doesn't know how she lost weight. She just woke up one day and it was gone. Sounds like she was in a coma.
One of them has been eating vegetables and shredded wheat. So far she's lost 30 pounds.
One of the girls had her stomach stapled.
So far I haven't felt the need to take any of these drastic measures.
Each year I just buy a bathing suit one size larger.

[THE SHORTER VERSION]   By Kathy Perry

IT'S OKAY BY ME IF IT'S OKAY BY YOU

Amy and I were bad this week. We both try to lose weight, or watch what we eat.

My husband always laughs at us because it seems he usually catches us literally with our hand in the cookie jar.

We love to bake, and of course, they are never "diet" cookies or cupcakes.

Now you can even buy microwave cakes. That used to be an excuse. I don't have time to bake or clean up the mess. Now you just stick it in the microwave, then eat the cake and, burn the pan. Amy and I made a pact. We decided we would buy fruit and start drinking more water or milk. No more pop or cookies and cakes.

All week we ate bananas and oranges or apples. We drank water instead of pop.

That is, until we stopped at the store to pick up a few things we needed and they already had Easter candy displayed. We picked up a box of chocolate marshmallow eggs and, of course, a box of little pink "peeps." We looked at each other and started to giggle. At the same time we said to each other, "it's okay by me, if it's okay by you."

[THE SHORTER VERSION] By Kathy Perry

NOW YOU KNOW

My sister always makes fun of me because I "forget" things.

I was sitting in front of the post office, and couldn't remember where I was going next.

I walk out in the kitchen, open the refrigerator, stand there for a few seconds then remember I came to the kitchen to get the scissors.

I walk into the family room and just stand there.

My kids remind me, "a mind is a terrible thing to waste."

I go to the grocery store with a list (a list that took several days to write), only to discover I can't find the list.

I try to buy clothes for my son, but I can't remember the sizes.

I open my mouth to speak and nothing comes out.

My husband and I watched a silly movie that Steve Martin was in and when the phone books came out he called his mother because he was so excited that his name was in the book. I was just about that excited about a little return address stamp I ordered. I was expecting Fate's Office Supply to call everyday, but they didn't.

Last night my husband handed me the stamp. Your sister has had this for sometime, she just forgot to tell you.

When I got home I called my sister. She was hysterical, "You know how much that little stamp meant to me," I said.

"Well," she began, "remember last week when I called you almost everyday and told you I had something to tell you, but I couldn't remember what it was---- "Now you know!"

[THE SHORTER VERSION] By Kathy Perry

IT'S LARRY, DARRELL AND DARRELL

The next time one of my children tells me they want a pet, excuse me, I had a lapse of memory.

What they tell me is that if I let them have a dog, cat, or bird, they will do all the work. They will pay for all the food. They will pay the vet bills. In fact, I won't even know the pets are in the house.

Not only do I know they are in the house, they are driving me crazy.

It started with one cat a few years ago. She had children and that cat had children. I have tried to give them away as birthday presents, Christmas presents, and now as my last hope, with Valentine's Day just a few days away, I'm going to wrap little bows, little red bows around their necks. It has become a mission, a quest! I've decided to put a kitten in each of my kids room. As long as the cat has food and water-the kids will never know the cat is in there. That is of course unless one of them moves.

If I do put those cats in the kids rooms, I'll need to prepare myself for the fact I may not see them until spring.

My girlfriend called the other day and asked me if I was having any luck.

I said, "Well, I've only got three left."

She replied, "That's wonderful, which three?"

"You know, It's Larry, Darrell and Darrell!

[THE SHORTER VERSION] By Kathy Perry

THE FEET HAVE IT

Several years ago, I fell down the stairs and hurt my back, so back pain is not uncommon for me.

Sometimes during the night my back will ache because I have been in one position too long. Usually, because my little dog, KoKo has fallen asleep beside me and I don't want to wake him. Once I can move around and get comfortable again I normally fall back to sleep.

The other night my back started to hurt in a different place. It was an unusual pressure type of pain. The pain kept waking me all night long. At one point, I thought maybe I should get up and sit in my rocker for a while. The pain seemed to go away when I woke up and moved. By dawn's early light I finally realized what was causing my "pain." A few weeks ago our portable television stopped working. So, we moved a console television into our bedroom. My husband can't see the TV when he's on his side of the bed. So several nights he lays at the foot of the bed.

The night that I was awakened by pain all night was one of the nights he had fallen asleep at the foot of the bed—his feet firmly planted on my back.

[THE SHORTER VERSION] *By Kathy Perry*

FAT PEOPLE REBEL

I think last week I had the worst day of my life. The very day I gave birth to my son, I got weighed at the hospital. Last week I got weighed and I weighed three pounds more than I did when I was nine months pregnant!

I have been able to hide it, tuck it, or squeeze it. But not anymore. I have two chins, and they both move when I laugh.

I've had to admit that I have no will power when it comes to food. The longest I've been able to stay on a diet was two days. That was 15 years ago when we were on vacation and I was locked inside a cabin in the woods with a sick child.

Everyone I know is on a diet. Most of my friends work out every day. I used to work out but I can't find my exercise tape. Besides, who wants to look like Richard Simmons. I've set new goals for myself. I can't wait for Roseann Barr's video. She's a woman after my own heart!

[THE SHORTER VERSION]   *By Kathy Perry*

IT'S IN MY ROOM

When she was about 13 years old, Julie used to come home from school and every day she would take her anger out on me. She used to throw things at me. Just small things, like her pencils, an eraser or a comb. According to her, everything that was unpleasant or completely wrong in her life was my fault. It was my fault that she didn't have dark hair, or brown eyes. It was my fault she didn't need glasses or braces on her teeth. It was my fault that her best friend (that day) didn't want to be her best friend any more.

It was my fault that we didn't have a dog named Daisy. It was my fault she had a "stupid" brother instead of a sister she could do things with.

One day she came home, threw her pencil in my direction and just started screaming. I just stood there and listened until she got to the part about "and another thing mother, you never do anything for me."

On that particular day, I reminded her that I did quite a few things for her every day---one of them being her laundry. On that day I informed her she would be doing her own laundry from that day forward.

So for the last six or seven years she has done her own laundry. A few weeks ago I asked to borrow one of her sweaters. Since I wore it I decided to wash it for her.

We have hard water so when I wash white clothes I use an additive to remove rust from the water and it keeps our white clothes white.

The sweater I borrowed from my daughter was off-white, but the sweater I pulled out of the dryer was bright white. I knew she would be very angry with me. I worried all day about how to tell her. Finally, I decided just to hold it up in front of me when she came home. She walked in the door, I held it up and she said, "Oh, thanks Mom for washing my white sweater. I

THE SHORTER VERSION
By Kathy Perry

wanted to wear that one tonight. The one you wore is off-white, it's upstairs in my room."

[THE SHORTER VERSION]   By Kathy Perry

I TOLD YOU SO

The other day I needed my son to help me pick up a bike. When he came home from work I asked him to go with me because it wouldn't fit in the back of my car. I really needed to use his truck.

After arguing with him for about four or five minutes about why he couldn't go with me, he finally said, "Oh, just take my truck. You can load the bike in it yourself, can't you?"

Of course I can, I thought to myself, I'm not helpless. While driving out of the driveway I was thinking angry thoughts about why he should have come with me. After all I've given him the best years of my life. And I thought of all the sacrifices I have made for him.

I was out on the highway trying to get the truck in some gear, and I realized his truck has no cruise control, no air conditioning, and no muffler.

I made it to my girlfriend's house and we loaded the bike in the back of his truck.

Come on in, she smiled, and have a diet Coke.

"I'd love to but he has to be at work by 4 and I promised him I would be right back."

Even though it's only about a 10 minute drive, I dutifully went back out to his truck to leave her house.

I put the key in the ignition and tried to start it. It wanted to start, but I remembered hearing him talk about the starter causing some problems.

I knew he would be sort of upset, but I called him anyway.

"Hi, I can't get your truck started, do you think you could have your sister bring you over here?"

Well, let me tell you, he was more than a little upset. "I can't believe this Mom, I'm going to be late for work and it's all your fault."

THE SHORTER VERSION
By Kathy Perry

"Look, sweetheart, I do believe I asked you several times to bring me, it's not like I stole your truck in the middle of the night."

"Okay, just push it and I know it will start."

"What!?" "How am I supposed to push it?"

There was a long silence on his end of the phone.

"Mom, just get in the truck and have Ellie push it with her hands. That's how I get it started all the time."

By now I'm starting to get really upset with him.

"Look, maybe you haven't noticed, but neither of us is 16 anymore. And besides I have a bike I can just ride home and leave your truck here and you can figure out how to get it home."

And when my son got there, he made his sister push his truck while he was steering. He shouted "get it up to 30 mph and we'll be in business." With that he popped the clutch and drove home.

[THE SHORTER VERSION] By Kathy Perry

MAN OR HIS BEST FRIEND

Did you ever try to sleep while someone was snoring beside you? My husband says he has (he probably means his mother).
If I fall asleep first he usually doesn't wake me up, but if something else wakes me up his loud snoring keeps me awake.
One night not too long ago, I kept waking up.
I pulled on his pillow-just a little bit, and he rolled over. He stopped snoring long enough for me to fall back asleep.
What seemed like a few minutes later the snoring woke me again.
So this time I shoved him. He rolled over and again I was able to fall back asleep before he started snoring again.
The next time he woke me I so angry I thought I'd stuff a sock in his mouth.
When I turned the light on to find something to stuff in his mouth, I realized I'd made a big mistake.
Every time I moved around on the bed I woke the dog. And when I woke him-he stopped snoring! I put him in the basement and slept the rest of the night.

[THE SHORTER VERSION] *By Kathy Perry*

COMMUNITY HARP

Have you ever gotten out of bed, just knowing the day might not go well? Well, my day was minor compared to a friends' day.

When I tried to brush my teeth this morning, someone had already used my toothbrush. And knowing my family as I do, I could only imagine what they had used it for. The first thing that came to mind was they probably brushed the dog's teeth, cleaned the hamster cage, cleaned a ring, or dropped it in the toilet. Needless to say, I retired that toothbrush. My daughter house sits for friends occasionally, and the other day was "one of those days."

The lady decided to sell her upright piano. When the buyers came to pick up the piano, they hadn't been able to find a truck to haul it in. So my daughter's friend offered to loan them hers. Everyone suggested they tie the piano securely, but the buyers said they would drive carefully. The buyers pulled out of the driveway slowly. They returned with the truck in about ten minutes. My daughter was hysterical listening to her friend recount her story.

"I knew they lived more than a half hour away and they couldn't be back so soon." "What happened," she asked the buyers.

"Well," the buyer scratched his head, "it seems as though when we turned the corner the piano went one way and the truck went the other. The piano kind of split in two. There's a big pile of kindling and right beside it looks like a harp."

My daughters' friend said, "We could invite people over to play the community harp, although they may have to lie on their back in the ditch."

The buyer shook his head and said, "Yeah, but there's not a scratch on your truck."

[THE SHORTER VERSION] *By Kathy Perry*

GRANDMA KNEW

My grandmother used to tell me that my life would never be dull. I never understood her insight, until recently.

She used to laugh at the things I would say and the things I would do.

I wonder if Grandma knew that I would have a son who would try to store a "dead animal" in the freezer.

One evening while enjoying the solitude of an otherwise explosive environment, black smoke would come billowing out of the wood burner, filling the entire house with smoke. It resembled the smog in Los Angeles. We could have hung meat in any room of the house to be cured.

Maybe she knew that one day I would have a cat who carries dog food all over the house. She bats it around on the floor and then eventually drops it in some one's shoe, as its final resting place.

The most fun of all is watching my husband squirm every year. He can never remember our anniversary or my birthday. They are only two days apart. So every year at the beginning of the week I start getting cards. The kids and I take bets to see if I'll get a birthday card or an anniversary card first.

[THE SHORTER VERSION] *By Kathy Perry*

FAIR WEATHER TRAINERS

Just recently my husband decided we would try to "get in shape" together.

"Yeah," he said, "when you work out together it's always easier."

So we started out with a diet. While I was talking to him about several diets I had heard about recently, he disappeared to the kitchen and brought back caramel corn.

Later we tried jogging. That lasted almost 15 minutes-longer than the diet.

Next we tried walking. Now that lasted several days (until it started raining). We are fair weather trainers.

Our next plan of attack was bicycling, but one of them had a flat tire, so he didn't get them out of the garage. He said, "hey, I've seen you and Amy do that 20-minute workout let's try that." He decided that was just for women and we needed to do something "together." We decided the only thing left was a rowing machine. So we jumped into the car and drove to Marion. When we got home we took it all out of the box, eager to assemble it and start rowing. As we pulled the last piece out of the box, I noticed we didn't have any nuts or bolts.

"I'd better drive back to Marion," he replied.

I heard him pull in the driveway.

"After the salesman opened two boxes," he started, "there weren't any nuts and bolts in either of those----then we realized we had everything we needed."

He followed me to the living room where the fully-assembled rowing machine sat.

"You realize if we had bought that thing in Mansfield I would have come back with divorce papers in my hand."

[THE SHORTER VERSION] *By Kathy Perry*

THE SWEEPER

I think the same person who invented fold up maps also invented artificial Christmas trees.
When you take that tree out of the box, the box shrinks.
There is no way "that" tree came out of "that" box. And where did I store all that stuff all year? Right at the moment its sitting in the hall because the closet it came out of is full of toys and clothes and boxes that I swear weren't there several weeks ago.
I recruited everyone to help me put things away this year.
Amy kept telling me she knew we were putting away more decorations than we got out. I was so anxious to take the tree down so we could clean the house and try to get everything back to "normal."
After we took the tree down and put all the decorations away I realized how empty the house looked. That was the day my husband called me from work. I could tell by the panic in his voice that something was wrong.
"Well," he began, " I realized on the way to work this morning what a mistake I made."
I had no idea what he was talking about.
"Before I left this morning," he explained, "I told the kids to clean their rooms."
"Well, that is wonderful! I want them to clean their rooms."
"But you don't understand, if they run the sweeper in there before they pick up the junk on the floor they will break the sweeper."
"Oh, that!" "Not to worry---neither one of them know where we keep the sweeper."

[THE SHORTER VERSION] *By Kathy Perry*

DON'T BLAME ME

We were discussing the fact that we are going to have to invest in a new dryer. The one we have just isn't working the way it's supposed to.

We were laughing about the times when my husband first started helping me with the laundry. Several sweaters with "dry clean only" got laundered. They became "doggie sweaters." Then we had the problem with color safe. My son was the only one who really complained about the pink underwear.

His next lesson in laundry was learning not to dry towels with sweaters or slacks unless you like fuzz balls.

I started to blame him for ruining a load of towels last week when I realized the dryer went nuts. The delicate cycle became the normal cycle and the normal cycle became fry. The clothes were so hot when they came out of the dryer they could almost burn your hands.

We were watching TV when Julie came storming into the family room clutching her new sweater vest in her fist. "Okay, which one of you should I thank for ruining my vest?"

"Well, honey, you know the dryer has been on the fritz this week and it overheats."

She glared at me and held the vest in front of her. "The dryer didn't turn it pink, Kathy."

[THE SHORTER VERSION] By Kathy Perry

SISTERLY LOVE

For as long as I can remember my sister, Pat, has always shared with anyone she can get to listen to her, the stupid things I do.

Like the time I was standing on the counter and tried to move a little step stool with my foot. It hadn't been secured on the sides so consequently when I stepped on it, it collapsed and I fell from the counter to the floor.

I lost my balance, fell against the drawers and slid down the handles. Both my feet were twisted like pretzels around the collapsed ladder. I knew immediately that nothing was broken and my daughter and I were hysterical.

Or like the time I "sort of" caught my panty hose on fire. I normally have several pair in the linen closet, but that morning the only pair I had was the pair I had worn the night before and they weren't completely dry. In a panic, I slid each leg, one at a time, over the end of the hair dryer. I temporarily forgot about the automatic shut off.

When the hair dryer shut off I realized they were not going to get any dryer. When I put them on there was a large hole in the knee where they had actually melted. I searched my closet for the longest dress I own.

The other day my sister and I were sitting in my car talking, waiting for a light to change. I turned to look out the window and when I turned back she was no longer "sitting" beside me. She was lying beside me, with tears of laughter rolling down her cheeks. She had pushed the lever to recline the seat, but because she is recovering from surgery she couldn't stop the seat herself, so she was completely reclined.

If I didn't love her I would have left her like that!

THE SHORTER VERSION
By Kathy Perry

FREE INSIDE

When he was little, my son used to pick out the kind of cereal he wanted by what was offered inside. Before he could read he enlisted the help of his sister. The two of them used to stand at the cereal aisle for a long time trying to decide which box had the best offer inside.

I always told them, "Now when we get home I don't want you digging around in the cereal box for the prize."

They always assured me they would eat every last morsel in the box, that not an ounce of cereal would be wasted. While I was struggling with bags of groceries, just lugging them from the car to the house, those little angels already had the cereal boxes open.

My son would usually dump the cereal into large mixing bowls until he found his prize, which was never on the top, but always at the very bottom of the box. He would usually play with the little car, truck, airplane or whatever happened to be in the box that week, and the entire box of cereal would still be sitting in the mixing bowls.

When I remember I try to dump it back in the cereal box, so it won't get stale. Most of the time I would forget, the cereal would go stale, and my son would not eat it.

I thought those days were gone forever, and that I would have to wait until I had grandchildren to deal with someone going through the boxes again. For the past several months my son has been feeding the cat, without any prompting from me.

I thought it was unusual, but I didn't say anything. The cat loved being fed two or three times a day. The other day I realized why he has been feeding her.

The brand of cat food I buy has an advertisement on the outside of the bag, "Free inside, collectible coin."

[THE SHORTER VERSION]   *By Kathy Perry*

WHEN IS WEDNESDAY

I have always admired women who could dress their children in cute little outfits, especially little girls with ribbons in their hair. I admire them because I used to try to dress my children in cute little outfits. The problem I always had was by the time I got the second one ready the first one looked like a little refugee. You know, like the ones you see in the magazine that you always want to send money to. My daughter used to rip the ribbon out of her hair just to see if they could retie them the way they were. My son used to cut his own hair, well parts of it. Usually just one side, or the front. I used to think I was the one who was disorganized.

I remember how they used to beg me to let them pack their lunches. Years later I found out they ate the Twinkies or Ho Ho's on the bus on the way to school. They sold their sandwich, and left the bag of potato chips on the seat.

A friend called the other day to tell me of her dilemma. I told her a long time ago she's going to make herself crazy with organization. In fact most of the time I get a headache just listening to her schedules. It seems she decided to give each of her four children a list of activities and jobs she had assigned for the following week. She sat down with them individually and went over the plan, asking each of them if they had any questions. They all seemed to understand what was expected of them, and each of them scurried off to another part of the house to play.

Her youngest son, however, disappeared. She searched outside and in the garage, and then in the basement. None of the other kids had seen him either. Finally she looked in his room. She found him there but he was lying across his bed sobbing uncontrollably.

She sat on the edge of his bed put her arms around him, "Bennie, what's the matter?"

THE SHORTER VERSION *By Kathy Perry*

He looked up through his tears, "Mommy, you told me to remind you of something next Wednesday, but I don't know when Wednesday is."

[THE SHORTER VERSION] By Kathy Perry

ON HIS OWN

Now that he is almost grown, my son reminds me all the time that he really doesn't need me to do anything anymore.

I suppose the time comes in every mothers life when it's time to shove them out of the nest. I really don't need to hear him remind me that he doesn't need me anymore.

Sometimes I have to laugh. He's been doing his own laundry for several years now, because one day he told me that I never do anything for him. I told him he was right. And the next day when he started yelling because he didn't have any clean jeans, he realized laundry was one of the things I wasn't doing for him anymore.

According to him, any moron can do laundry. I remember his words and the stern look on his face. How difficult can it be to throw clothes in the washer then throw them in the dryer. I might have added, and then throw them on your floor, but I didn't. He didn't want to take the time to sort the clothes. He even bragged to me about saving time and money by only doing one or two loads instead of four or five. Imagine my surprise when he had blue underwear. He washed his jeans, flannel shirts, socks and underwear all together. He also washed towels with sweaters, and then wanted to know how to get those little "lint balls" off his sweaters.

Now he says nicer things to me, like "will you put my clothes in the dryer, or do you think you can fix this shirt? It used to be green with white stripes and now it's lime green all over."

I think if I kept a journal about all the "nice" things he has ever said to me, the other day would have been a classic. He needed to type a report. He wanted me to type it, but I didn't have time at the exact moment he wanted me to do it. "Oh, just forget it he shouted, I'll do it myself."

At first I told him if he touched my computer I would saw off his fingers.

THE SHORTER VERSION
By Kathy Perry

"Look Mom, how difficult can it be to use your stupid computer. Besides I've had computers at school. Anybody can use one."

"But, I protested, "you don't even know how to open a document."

He yelled, "Can't you just show me?"

You have to realize he wanted me to show him how to operate my computer in the five minutes before I had to leave.

I showed him which drive to insert the floppy diskette and gave him the password. I went to the other room to get my purse and coat. When I came back to my desk he had three errors and he wasn't able to open the document he wanted. I got him into the document and then told him I had to leave.

"Wait," he shouted, "before you leave, could you just show me how to turn it off?"

[THE SHORTER VERSION] By Kathy Perry

JUST CARRY ON

I don't know about your kids, but when my kids are sick the entire world stops. Now we aren't talking anything major here, just a simple cold or sore throat. The kind that just takes seven days to disappear on it's own.

When they walk in the door on the first day of their illness it starts with "Mom, I'm sick. Will you fix some soup for me?"

And my response in my June Cleaver voice, "You do sound like you might be coming down with something."

It's downhill from there.

As I'm cooking chicken soup they are in their room sorting through all the things they may need for the next 48 hours.

They will need a favorite blanket, several pillows, several boxes of Kleenex, a bell to ring for my attention in case I'm in the same room and a bull horn if I happen to be in another part of the house. While they are in recovery, it is my responsibility to prepare their favorite meals, (feed a cold). They usually take the time to scrawl a list of requests from the grocery and drug stores.

No matter what my plans are for that day or even that particular moment, I will be canceling them, because "I could be dying Mom."

After they were all healthy and back at school and work I came down with the same thing they had, except I had bronchitis.

They still came home from work and school and expected me to have the laundry done, dinner on the table and cookies in the cookie jar.

I'm better now. The only thing they noticed during my illness was that we ran out of milk. Don't worry about me kids, I'll be just fine.

[THE SHORTER VERSION] *By Kathy Perry*

STRESS MANAGEMENT

Just about every magazine I pick up these days has an article about stress or stress management. Although most of the articles do address the problems of stress, I'm not sure those people who write the articles have teenage children.

Stress took on a whole new meaning when both my children reached "teen years."

For instance, stress to me means coming home on Monday (the worst day of the work week for me) pulling the car into the garage, shutting off the motor and resting, wanting to take a deep breath before the evening starts. However, before I can unbuckle my seat belt, two of my children are at either door of my car. One wants to know what's for supper, while the other one wants a ride for he and one of his friends to a movie.

Pardon me, I tell them, I don't know "what's for supper" and no movie tonight—it's a school night.

Neither of them is happy with the answer they got, so they decide to fight with each other.

I change my clothes, throw a load in the washer, and head to the kitchen. Before I can start dinner I have to wash dishes because everyone had a snack when they came home. With dishes done and dinner on the table, I asked my son to take the clothes out of the washer, put them in the dryer and start another load.

We all sit down, eat dinner, the kids are still fighting about important world affairs like who did the dishes last night.

After dinner, while they are yelling and clearing the table, I wanted to wash one more load of clothes.

I opened the lid of the washer, the one my son loaded, to find it loaded with five pairs of his socks!

Now that's what I call stress.

[THE SHORTER VERSION] *By Kathy Perry*

I'M ASHAMED OF YOU MOM

My son can no longer hurl the fat jokes at me. Amy and I have gotten serious about our exercising. We're going two nights a week now to work out.

Jason can't come in the kitchen anymore and call it the sweatshop. Now when I run through the house, he can't shout, "Hey Mom, that tremor just measured 7.2 on the Richter scale! Someday soon we are going to burn our stretch pants with the elastic waistbands.

We'll be able to have a full-length mirror in the bathroom again. I should be able to see my thighs by summer.

It's pretty embarrassing when a seven-year-old can keep up with a ---well, her mother.

Amy doesn't miss a beat! That kid still has energy when we get home at night. The other night I was just trying to breathe. I looked over at Amy. She was moving her arms and keeping up with the instructor. In fact, she didn't look any different than she would have if she had been sitting on the couch beside me at home.

Amy could probably conduct an exercise class, but the only people who could keep up with her would be other first graders or their teacher.

One night, just to throw her off the track, I slid over beside her in line. "Hey Amy, you wanna go to Porters for some ice cream when we finish this work out?"

She put her hand on her hip and pointed with her finger. "Get back in line, Mom, you have to finish this work out." Then in a thoroughly disgusted little voice, she continued, "ice cream! I'm ashamed of you, Mom!"

[THE SHORTER VERSION] *By Kathy Perry*

HAPPY ANNIVERSARY DEAR

Since my husband and I have conflicting schedules, we almost have to make an appointment to see each other. It's almost like dating.

"Let's see, could you work me in next Thursday afternoon?"

"Okay, then how about the next Thursday?"

And so it goes from week to week. On several occasions his day off turned out to be my busiest day, the day I didn't get home until 8:30 or 9:00 that night. We were becoming a family without him. He had no idea what any of us were doing.

For a while I wrote notes to him, but it was taking too long, and usually when I finally had time to write, I was fighting sleep.

Not too long ago he started getting up about 20 minutes earlier to spend some time with me in the morning before I left for work.

He usually fixes a cup of Suisse Mocha for me, and a cup of coffee for himself.

The other night was an unusually late night for him and because our anniversary was near, I wanted to do something special for him.

So that morning I made my own Suisse Mocha and his cup of coffee and had it waiting for him in the already sun-filled dining room.

He always says it takes a good cup of coffee to wake him every morning.

He smiled at me and took a sip of the hot coffee. Then his eyes crossed and his lip curled.

"What? I made that coffee the same way I make my Suisse Mocha."

He tried to be nice. "I only put one teaspoon of coffee in a cup."

"Well, you've got enough for three cups then."

[THE SHORTER VERSION] *By Kathy Perry*

DO NOT ENTER

Since my children were at least five, six or maybe even seven I have not allowed friends or family to enter their rooms without first having a tetanus shot.

When they were younger, I used to clean their rooms every Saturday morning. I would pull a week's worth of clothes along with one pair of underwear out from under their beds. I would pry Popsicle sticks off the carpet and gum off the nightstand. It normally took half a roll of paper towels to wipe the graffiti off the walls. Today it's not much different except I'm afraid I'll have a stroke if I enter their rooms.

The only time I even bother is if I happen to be upstairs and I notice "things" falling out of their doors. I usually pick it up so the dog doesn't trip and fall down the stairs. None of them remember if there is carpet on the floor. The dog will only go in one of their rooms.

My daughter has lost earrings, the title to her car and shoes--- all lost in her room—so imagine my surprise the other day.

My husband had been suffering terribly from a toothache. So, when my daughter came home, they were discussing the alternatives.

She advised him he would probably have to have his tooth pulled.

"Wait here!" she yelled over her shoulder. She was back in two seconds with her prize.

"It's a tooth I had pulled when I was in eighth grade!.

[THE SHORTER VERSION] *By Kathy Perry*

THE MOUNTAIN MAN

My son in all his infinite wisdom never ceases to amaze me. He only wants to talk about guns or traps. He has hundreds of gun magazines everywhere. He dreams of moving to Montana where he and his faithful dog can live in solitude in a one-room log cabin. He will be able to "live off the land."
I'm not sure what he'll do with the "day's catch" because he won't need a freezer or refrigerator because "it's always cold in Montana."
I know that living in a one-room house with a dirt floor won't bother him because he isn't aware that he has carpet on his bedroom floor.
Sometimes I worry, because at times he still seems so young and I'm not sure he's ready for the world out there. He tells me that he'll be moving in just a few months, as soon as he graduates.
Well, my faith has been restored in him. Just two nights ago you should have seen his cute little face when I brought him a kite, and what a sight, watching my mountain man and his dog fly his kite!

[THE SHORTER VERSION] *By Kathy Perry*

X-RAY VISION

A few weeks ago my daughter was on a roll. Not the good kind. One night she and her brother decided to drive into town for something to eat. Right before they left she smashed her finger in a window she was trying to close.

The dress she ordered for a wedding was too big and it was too late to send it back. The shoes she ordered needed to be dyed and she was afraid the dye wouldn't come in time.

Then something happened to her tires. She decided she would bake chocolate chip cookies one night. I really don't know what she did, because normally her chocolate chip cookies are wonderful. That night she burned the first batch and the second batch was not baked in the center.

Earlier that evening she tried to dye her shoes. She had instructed each of us not to touch them. She was upset with everyone. She left them on the floor in the family room on a newspaper. She returned to the kitchen to finish baking cookies. Her brother walked over and picked up one of her newly-dyed shoes.

From the kitchen she shouted at her brother. He looked at me and grinned, "She saw me through the wall."

[THE SHORTER VERSION] *By Kathy Perry*

CONGRATULATIONS GRADUATES

I REMEMBER THE DAY THEY HANDED HER TO ME IN THE HOSPITAL. She was pink and wrinkled. Everybody said she had my nose and her dad's ears. I didn't think she resembled anyone I had ever known. In fact, I kept checking the identification bracelet on her arm to make sure it matched mine.

I dressed her a few days later in "real" clothes for the big trip home. I knew all the grandmas and grandpas would be there waiting for us. And they were. All trying to decide which side of the family she resembled.

Several months later the little cherub started walking about in a walker. The second day she was in that walker she managed to pull every leaf off my rubber tree one at a time. She would laugh with such delight as she held up "another treasure." Finally all I had left was a stick in a large pot.

It seemed only a few months later, she was learning to ride her bike. One day after another fall I counted 31 stars and stripes bandages on her knee.

We moved on to kindergarten and Brownies.

The next few years she dragged me to PTA, and I always had to go because if her class had the most parents there, they would be rewarded with a taco party. If I didn't go, I would have been the only parent in the class who wasn't there.

Just a few more years passed before that same little girl in the walker was now driving her own car.

She fell in and out of love every other week.

My grandma always said, "You won't believe how fast they grow up. Grandma used to tell me that when I complained about washing diapers or following her through a room to pick up her toys.

Grandma was right. Yesterday, today and tomorrow. My "little girl" graduates from high school next week.

Congratulations, Julie Ann Rogers, Class of '86. I love you.

[THE SHORTER VERSION] *By Kathy Perry*

HAPPY FATHER'S DAY

This year on Father's Day, I wanted to get my dad something special. When I asked him what he wanted he said, "nothing." It's hard to buy anything for someone who already has everything he wants.

I remember growing up, my dad was always there. Not necessarily "with" me, but he was at work or out in the field on a tractor. When I was little, I remember thinking when I grow up I would marry my dad, because he was the strongest, smartest, bravest and most handsome man I knew.

The older I grew, the dumber he got. By the time I was a teenager, I was surprised he could even get his shoes on the right feet.

He would yell at me for drag racing in his car (I always wondered how he found out). He was always mad at me 'for no reason'. He finally started to outgrow his "stupid stage."

The older I got, the smarter he got. I've been so lucky to have a strong, smart, brave and handsome man for a father. I don't think my father realizes how important he is to all of us.

If we need a plumber, locksmith, carpenter, electrician, mechanic, gardener, or someone to make homemade ice cream, we all call him. He always grumbles that he can't do it. Usually as soon as he hangs up the phone he reaches for his hat and calls his dog and they are on their way.

How can you really say thank you to a man who has given you a lifetime of friendship, love, a lot of yelling but mostly just being there when you needed him. From your entire family, we say thank you Dad.

Happy Father's Day, John R. Neff.
I love you, Dad.

THE SHORTER VERSION
By Kathy Perry

TRUST ME

For years I have brought home literature about smoking. How to quit, facts about how he's killing himself, and the pitfalls of second hand smoke. My husband won't quit. He wheezes when he exerts himself, he coughs every time he wakes up. He's short of breath when he climbs stairs and he has chest pains when he gets nervous. And the best part—the very best part is that he pays over $365 a year for that disgusting habit. I've told him all the things the kids and I will do when I'm a widow. But that doesn't stop him either. So we all decided to stop nagging. He'll never quit.

The other day when he came home from work he had a little sore on his lip. "What happened to your lip?" I asked. He just looked at me, mumbled something under his breath and walked away from me.

My curiosity was aroused, so I continued my interrogation.

"You really don't want to know," he said in a stern voice.

"Yes, I do," I nodded.

"Well," he began, "I sort of burned it with a cigarette."

I screamed, "You stuck the wrong end in your mouth after you lit it and burned your lip?" I was hysterical!

He sheepishly nodded his head.

"Don't worry, dear, your secret is safe with me."

[THE SHORTER VERSION] *By Kathy Perry*

WE CAN DO IT

Well girls we finally did it. That's right, we finally proved we could do it.

We've been able to "show them" we can "bring home the bacon," we can fry it, we can eat it, then we can clean up. We proved we could do it all.

Now that I've proven to myself I can be Super Mom, I've decided to make my husband a deal. He can earn the money, and I can spend it.

Of course, he'll say, you deserve to stay home. I can hear him now.

No more getting up at 5:30 for me. I'll cook breakfast for my children the night before. They can eat before they go to bed. I'll cook a little gruel. It will help them develop character.

I can sleep in everyday. I'll hire a cleaning lady. Then I'll hire someone to grocery shop and cook. I'll finally be able to catch up on my sleep. I'll be able to read all the magazines and books I've been saving for my retirement.

I looked at my husband and he was just sitting in the dining room at the table and he kept handing me hundred dollar bills. I heard the timer go off on the stove and I started to walk into the kitchen, then I woke up. I rolled over and looked at the clock, it was 5:30---time to get up---have lots to do.

[THE SHORTER VERSION] By Kathy Perry

SAVE YOUR BREATH

The famous Danish philosopher Kierkegaard once wrote, "During the first period of a man's life, the greatest danger is not to take the risk."
I've always tried to instill in my children to venture out. Always try new things. It doesn't matter if you fail because you tried.
I'm beginning to wonder if any of the great philosopher's had teenage children.
'Since birth I have tried everything to motivate my children, to stimulate them. My son is motivated. I'm not sure by what yet, but I'm getting closer. He can be a genius about events in history, or the parts of a gun. He can disassemble and reassemble a gun in record time, even those tiny little screws. But change the sweeper bag, or turn on the dryer, he's brain dead.
I think I'll write a book myself on teen-aged motivation.
I will entitle it, "Save Your Breath."

[THE SHORTER VERSION] *By Kathy Perry*

A RAINY DAY

One of the guys I work with is young and single and always talking about all the money he spends. I guess he can do it because he works two other jobs and has no one else to spend his money on.

He could easily wear a different suit everyday of the week for two or three months. He has lots of shirts and coats and about 40 pairs of shoes. Everyone at Lazarus knows him on a first name basis. When he goes out for dinner it is nothing for him to blow $40 or $50 in an evening. He teases me all the time because I would rather shop at Dollar General than Lazarus.

Last week I was thrilled because I bought a new watch, a Timex and it was half price. I was so proud of my bargain I showed him the first thing in the morning. He showed me his Gucci, which cost more than my house.

He told me the other day that he just didn't know what to spend all his money on.

I suggested saving a little for a "rainy day." To which he replied, "My rainy days are over." Well, guess what-last week it poured.

His car blew up, his roommate moved out, the battery in his Gucci corroded---but my Timex is still ticking!

[THE SHORTER VERSION] *By Kathy Perry*

IT WAS LIKE THAT WHEN I GOT HERE

My cousin Kim, her husband Tom, and their baby T.J., were home for the weekend. We girls had the opportunity to have brunch. We all reminisced about days gone by.
There are 10 years between myself and Kim and 10 years between Kim's sister and my sister. Grandma always referred to them as the "little girls."
We thought of them as adorable doll babies. They were even better than Cabbage Patch kids.
We used to love to dress them up and the girls loved for us to put makeup on them. My dear, sweet uncle Bob, who was always so serious--- thought they looked like clowns. That usually didn't stop us.
Kim always loved to take bubble baths, so I would fill the tub to the top. My poor uncle Bob thought I would drown her.
We always loved to carry the girls, and my uncle used to remind us that the girls could walk.
I think the worst thing we ever did, was after we were both older Kim, who was five and I fifteen, loved for me to swing her around like an airplane. One year when we were at Grandmas' house for Christmas, I was swinging Kim and I got too close to the Christmas tree.
Kim's foot got caught in the garland and we pulled the tree over. Grandma always put a live tree up early, so by Christmas Day the tree was very dry.
All the needles fell off and most of the decorations. We stood the tree back up and tried to throw some of the decorations back on, and run over to the sofa so we could sit and act like we were just as surprised as our parents that all the needles and decorations had just fallen off the tree.
My sister tells me the reason my children say "it was like that when I got here," is because they inherited it.

[THE SHORTER VERSION] By Kathy Perry

THEY ARE ALL CRAZY

It is pretty hard to survive when you live with a bunch of comedians. I think I have been seeing too many articles about lost children, because the other night I dreamed my little dog Simon's picture was on a milk carton. Only another dog lover can appreciate how I feel about my little dachshund.
I told my husband about my horrible dream. At the time I thought he was being sympathetic.
When my daughter came home, my husband said "Did your Mom tell you about her dream?"
My daughter shook her head.
After I poured out my heart to her, I realized they were both laughing at me.
"Look you guys," I shouted, "I've had a bad day. First I dream someone kidnapped little Simon, and then my sister who is a comedian wants to charge me a stud fee because her cat, who was visiting us, happened to be a male, and now our cat is going to have kittens.
As I leaned back in the recliner to settle down for a few minutes, Julie asked me to bring her some yogurt.
I gave her a dirty look, but she begged me, so I finally got up and walked out to the kitchen. As I opened the refrigerator door, I could hear the laughter from the other room.
There as big as life, taped to the milk carton was Simon's picture.

THE SHORTER VERSION
By Kathy Perry

BOYS OR GILRS

The biggest difference between raising boys or girls is when you hear a loud crash from your daughter's room. A noise that resembles a dresser falling over, and you yell, "what's going on up there?" They always giggle and in their sweetest voice, "Nothing, Mom." However, if the same sound comes from your sons' room, he'll tell you "we just put the cat out on the roof to see if she could climb back in and it's really neat."

Little boys like to play with fish worms, let them crawl all through their fingers or tease their sister with them. Boys will let the dog lick their face, but they won't drink after their sister. The grubbier their jeans are indicates whether or not they've had a successful day. A clean pair of jeans would probably mean they "didn't have any fun."

You would be nominated for an academy award if you were able to talk your son into taking a bath.

Little girls change their clothes seven times a day, take a bubble bath about that many times and scream hysterically if a worm even darkens her door.

Little boys rarely give compliments unless they want something. Little girls are always trying to say something nice.

I remember once when Amy was only about three years old. She had been staring at me for a while. I finally asked her why. She replied, "'you know Mom, you're really pretty, except for your Woody Picker nose."

[THE SHORTER VERSION]   By Kathy Perry

VALENTINE REMEMBRANCE

While I was sitting at the dinning room table watching my five year old cut out hearts for Valentines Day, I remembered when I was little, probably in the second or third grade. We had a Valentine's Day party at school. A week before the party I went to grandma's house. She took me shopping for Valentine cards, white tissue paper and red construction paper. Grandma demonstrated her patience while I found that special box of cards which included a card for my teacher. After the shopping trip I begged grandma to give me one of her shoe boxes. It had to be just the right size.

When she finally consented, I cut out a little hole in the top of my new "mail box." I placed the little red hearts I had so carefully cut out all over the new white box. I took my "mailbox" home along with the box of Valentine cards. I went to work right away signing and addressing those little cards. I kept asking mom how to spell some of the names.

I tried to select a card I thought each person would love.

When I came home from school that day, I knew I was in love. Billy, Bobby and Johnny all gave me special cards. My little "mailbox" was tucked full of goodies, cookies, cards and candy hearts.

I said to my little five year old, "You know Amy, Valentine's Day is just a few days away. We have to make your Valentine's box and address the cards. "She tipped her head and replied, "Do you think I could do it myself this year, mom?"

I sure hope she lets me help.

[THE SHORTER VERSION] By Kathy Perry

MOTHER'S TAXI SERVICE

My girlfriend called to tell me she was so upset because her children don't appreciate her.

"The only time they know I'm alive is when they need me to drive them somewhere."

I thought to myself after we hung up what it would have been like without my children.

When I come home from work, the house would still look like it did when I left. No milk glasses half full on the coffee table or Twinkie wrappers on the end tables. When I climb into the shower there would be no rubber duckie or an inflatable ring for a rub-a-dub dollie. I wouldn't have to look for my shampoo or wonder who left the cap off my cream rinse which is now diluted. I would not have to look for my hot curlers or my curling iron.

The sink wouldn't have three globs of toothpaste smeared all over it and the toothpaste would have the cap on it.

My favorite blouse that I planned to wear to work today would not be rumpled in the laundry, because it also happens to be one of my daughter's favorites. There wouldn't be peanut butter and jelly smeared on the kitchen counter next to the open bread wrapper.

But then I would not have anyone to remind me to feed the dogs. I wouldn't have anyone to drive around. I suppose my life would be pretty boring. I would like to be bored for just a day.

[THE SHORTER VERSION] *By Kathy Perry*

GRANDMA'S TRUNK

Last week after my daughters pre-school teacher called to say she would be making a home visit, I thought what better time to start my spring cleaning.
I woke feeling very energetic and decided to start in the attic. That was my first mistake. I planned to deep clean, you know the way they do on television. Her mother-in-law visits and can see herself in the china, or wipes the top of the TV with a white glove on. My mother-in-law could write the constitution on top of my TV with a white glove.
I was in the attic when I located a truck that had belonged to my grandmother. It hadn't been opened for years.
In it were three generations of memorabilia. Grandmother's, my Mother's and mine. I found a dress of my grandmothers and a doll with a porcelain face, a pair of black high button shoes and some lace hankies.
I sat my coffee cup on the ledge of the windowsill and continued my search.
There were letters written to my grandmother by my grandfather and sheet music grandmother used to play for church. As I sat on my knees I could imagine grandmother wearing the silky dress I held in my hands.
As I filtered through the treasures, I was taken back in time. I could imagine riding in a Model-T Ford, or sitting on the swing on the front porch drinking iced tea or lemonade on a Sunday afternoon.
I found a corset that must have caused her great discomfort. No wonder in all the pictures of her she always had a three-inch waist.
In the bottom of the trunk, as I leaned over, I found their wedding picture. Both looking very regal and stoic.
I was jolted back to reality when someone slammed the door downstairs and shouted, "Mom, we're home."

[THE SHORTER VERSION] *By Kathy Perry*

I couldn't believe it, I had spent nearly two hours looking through that old trunk.
"I'm up here," I yelled.
My son bounced up the stairs and stood before me.
"What are you looking for mom?" he said as he walked over to the trunk and picked up the high button shoes.
"Did you used to wear these to school, mom?"
Of course I did, I thought to myself. The stagecoach was usually cold.

[THE SHORTER VERSION] *By Kathy Perry*

MODERN TECHNOLOGY

Last week one night, my husband decided it was time I learned to type with a word processor. He came home and said, "You know all the writers are using word processors now. I think it's time you put your typewriter away and learn to use a word processor."
He handed me five manuals to read and retorted, "Why don't you just sit down and relax and flip through those manuals. The salesman said, "Anyone can learn to use one of these things."
Besides, I think it will be fun to learn about new technology. "Come on, we'll do it together!"
He set everything up in the kitchen. He looked like a little boy opening Christmas presents. I haven't seen him so excited in a long time. After several days of listening to tapes and reading the manuals, I thought maybe he was right. I should try to use the word processor instead of my typewriter. After all, these are changing times. He's probably right about other writers using "modern equipment" too.
I sat down on the fourth day and started typing material from my latest novel. I was so proud of myself! I had completed ten pages and thought I would go back later to edit the material. Everything was all contained on that little diskette. It was close to dinnertime so I took the little diskette out of the computer and put it back in its jacket. When my husband came home he was so proud of me. He sat down to look at the material I had typed. When he put the little diskette in place and called it up, the error message read, "file not found."
So much for "modern technology," where's my typewriter?

[THE SHORTER VERSION] *By Kathy Perry*

THEY ALWAYS HELP

I believe there is a little imp living within the walls of my home. He must have an antenna to alert my children. As soon as I've finished cleaning the kitchen, put the dishes away and wiped the water spots from the sink, the antenna goes up and tells them they must be hungry for a snack. Let's go smear peanut butter on the counter. Use the same knife we spread the peanut butter to also spread jelly. Then leave it on the counter beside the open peanut butter and jelly jars beside the open bread wrapper.

After I've vacuumed the entire house and dusted, someone desides to brush the dog and comb the cat, in the house.

The minute they hear the disinfecting bubbles in the toilet---you guessed right.

When I finally have a chance to sit down after doing the laundry, I see the three of them march past me with laundry baskets piled full of their dirty clothes. They only drop globs of toothpaste in the bathroom sink after they are sure I've scoured it.

When it comes time to burn the trash, no one can ever find the matches. When I go out to burn it myself, volunteer fire departments come from three counties.

During our recent snowstorm, I asked my son to shovel the sidewalk. I couldn't open the back door due to the drifting snow. He shoveled it from the walk, but threw it in front of the garage door.

I came home from the doctor's office the other day, recovering from a nasty cold and the flu, he said "Go home Kathy, and go back to bed. Your children are old enough to help.

I replied, "They always do."

[THE SHORTER VERSION] *By Kathy Perry*

DID YOU SAY BOY GEORGE?

The other day my teen-aged daughter and her friends were laughing at me because I thought the name of a popular song was "Become a Comedian."
They were hysterical at my mistake. I love the singer's voice and when I inquired, they informed me his name is "Boy George."
Being from the early 18th century, "Boy George" had a wholesome ring to it. I imagined a clean cut young man with short blond hair. Probably blue eyes, too. He has such a mellow voice. Much to my chagrin, last week while watching the Grammy Awards, I had the opportunity to see "Boy George."
"Mom, come quick, here's your chance to see that wholesome star, it's Boy George."
I hurried to dry my hands and rushed into the family room.
"Well, where is he? I didn't rush in here to watch her."
The room filled with laughter.
"Mom, that IS Boy George," they shouted in unison.
I looked astonished.
"But that's a pretty little girl."
"Look again, Mom"
His eyebrows had a better arch than mine. His clothes were a little bit flashy. I think he was wearing a hat over his carefully braided hair. I watched as the words from that now familiar song flowed from his ruby red lips. Somehow, music just doesn't seem to be the same as when I was growing up. Now there's also Michael Jackson, another pretty one.
I told my daughter, I'm going to dress like a man, sing like a woman, and let the world guess. Who knows, maybe I'll be the next "Girl Kathy."

[THE SHORTER VERSION] *By Kathy Perry*

MY PUNK ROCK MOM

Why is it we as parents feel like idiots when our children become teenagers?

There have been days when they make me wonder how I've survived all these years.

Suddenly my clothes are "outdated," but they still end up in my daughter's closet.

The shoes I pick out look like "Grandma" shoes. I wish someone would explain why those same shoes are on the floor of her closet when I want to wear them. My jeans aren't the famous designer jeans that are "in," I'll bet if she was paying for them she would love the brand I wear. My hair is another story. How does she think I got "all that gray hair?" Sometimes they are embarrassed by the way I talk. Maybe this weekend when they want me to drive them to the Purple Indian, I'll say. "No, duh."

I could probably learn to speak their language if I really tried; but who would I talk to? I wonder what my children would think if they came home from school, and I was wearing a white tee shirt and jeans cut just below my knees, white bobby socks and white tennis shoes. I'd probably need some long earrings. I'd have to change the color of my hair, just in the front. Maybe green or orange.

I wonder if they would think their Mom was smarter if she was a punk rocker.

I remember when a young friend of mine told me her Mom used to be dumb, too, but she finally outgrew it.

[THE SHORTER VERSION] *By Kathy Perry*

WHERE'S THE HEDGE?

Did you ever wonder who's idea it was to weed the garden? I don't mind looking for the vegetables.
And what about the lawn? Why do we have to trim around everything? The fence doesn't look different after the weeds are gone. We have to prune the roses and the hedge. We have to rotate the tires. Why do we have to change the oil? Why can't we just add more?
Every week we spend half our paycheck on groceries, and the next week we have to do it again. We wash the dishes and the clothes just so we can dirty them.
We take a bath and wash our hair and do the same thing the next day.
I gave Simon a bath this afternoon so he could go back outside and roll in the remains of the fish Jason caught last week.
We diet so we can lose weight, so that when we go to the family reunion we can eat Aunt Helen's famous dessert. We cut our hair, just so it can grow. Windows, now there's another one.
You wash them every year and before you turn around it's time to do it again.
My list is endless. I could go on for hours.
I remember, just the other day I told my husband just how I felt.
I suggested to him that even though I felt that way he probably should trim the hedge. He said he understood exactly how I felt.
When I came home from the grocery store, the shrubbery was gone. He got out the chain saw and cut them to the ground. He looked so pleased as I walked out front to get a better look. There were about five piles of evergreen-EVERYWHERE!
He looked at me proudly and said, "I hope you weren't kidding about trimming the hedge?"

[THE SHORTER VERSION] *By Kathy Perry*

PIGS CAN'T CLIMB STAIRS

The other day Jason decided he'd like to be a farmer. A wise profession, I thought to myself. My father and grandfather were both farmers.

"I'd like to start off with a few pigs and maybe a cow, OK, Mom?"

"It's okay with me Jason, but where do you plan to keep these animals? I agreed to the hamster and then the cat and the dog. I even let you bring the goldfish home that you won at the fair. We don't have a barn, or even a utility building."

"Listen, Mom," he continued, "I've got the whole thing figured out. I thought I could keep a little pig either in my room or in the basement. Just until I get the money to build a pole barn."

"In your room!" I protested. "You've got to be kidding. Just last week your father was upset about the dog stealing his socks. How do you think he would feel about a pig running through the living room?"

"Mom, think how much money I can make. You know, for college. After I sell the first pig, I'll reinvest the money. I'll keep buying pigs and maybe a cow or two. But I'll just keep investing the money. I promise I won't buy any more model rockets."

"Do you realize how much it costs to feed livestock?" "I could tell he wasn't listening to me. "Not to mention if one of your little piggies gets sick."

"Don't worry Mom, just relax, I've got it figured out."

"Jason, I pleaded, "where are you going to keep this little pig?

"Nobody will have to know about it. I'll keep it in my room for a while. I'll just keep the door closed. Besides pigs can't climb stairs."

[THE SHORTER VERSION] By Kathy Perry

MIDDLE AGE BLAHS

This afternoon Amy asked me how soon she could start saying she is five and a half.
"You can say it now if you like," I smiled at her.
Her eyes were as big as saucers.
"I can't wait until school tomorrow. All the kids will be so surprised."
I tried to remember when I was five or six and how thrilled I was to reach the halfway mark.
I used to argue with my sister, who is three years younger. Her argument was that since her birthday is in April and mine in May, for several weeks I was only two years older than she. I remember how angry I used to feel because I thought she was right. At the time I felt there was a certain social stigma to being three years older.
Every time I pick up a magazine now there is an article about the middle age blahs. I didn't feel bad about middle age until I started reading those articles about wrinkles and age spots and a thousand different colors to change "ugly" gray hair.
Twenty years ago, I read articles on fashion and the latest hair styles. After that, it was articles on how to prepare baby formula.
Now I'm at the halfway mark. Middle age.
When I was 15, halfway meant over the hill. It was rocking chair time. I couldn't visualize my first gray hair or age spot.
When my sister called yesterday and said "So you've got a birthday coming up next week," I casually replied,
"Yes and by the way. I'm 39 and a half."

[THE SHORTER VERSION]   *By Kathy Perry*

AMY'S SUMMER JOB

Since everyone else is talking about a summer job, Amy decided she needs one too.

Her first project was to walk the dog. Since we live in the country, and the dogs walk themselves, she decided that would not be very profitable. Her next idea was to help me with the housework. After her third trip to the basement with an empty laundry basket, she decided that was too hard. Washing dishes seemed like a lot of fun. All those bubbles would almost be like a bubble bath. I think that was the day she decide to go into business for herself. She tried to devise a plan where the dishes would be her sole responsibility. The first day she did great, because no one was home to eat. Just a sandwich on the run. The next day, however, was a different story. There were breakfast dishes, dishes from lunch and dishes from dinner. Poor Amy looked at me and said, "Mom, this is too much for me, I'm just a little kid."

I was hoping she would learn a lesson in responsibility.

"How about if I help you Amy?"

"If you help me, do I still get to keep the money?"

"I think if I help you we should split the money."

I could tell she wasn't pleased with that decision. She was already planning the next big money maker.

Jason yelled as he stomped through the house. "Do you think you could pay me $40 if I cut the grass and do all the trim?"

"I think that seems fair, Jason."

Amy looked at me with her big blue eyes and tipped her head. "Do you think I could have $10 if I pick all the dandelions?"

[THE SHORTER VERSION] *By Kathy Perry*

THE LINE FORMS HERE

After living in a big city, I'd gotten used to waiting in long lines at the grocery store. Long lines at the drive thru window at the bank. Even long lines at the check out at the drug store. Not only was I used to the long lines, but I also learned to be impatient and in a hurry.

There was usually a two hour wait at the veterinarian's office, too. Even something as simple as a driver license renewal required waiting in a long line.

When I moved to a smaller community, I wasn't prepared. The first time I shopped at the grocery store, I automatically went to the end of the line. When I looked over to the next check out, I realized there was no one in her line. One of the ladies in the line was exchanging a recipe from her Aunt Bertha. I couldn't believe it. Didn't they know I was in a hurry?

When I took Simon to the vet for his summer booster shots, my sister prepared me. "You'll have to wait on Saturday, that's usually his busiest time." Remembering the usual two hour wait, I took a thick book. There was only lady waiting when Simon and I got there. Of course Simon tried to protect me from her fierce dog, which turned out to be a little pig.

I think I was in his office a total of 15 minutes. I was shocked when the vet offered to help each of us to our cars, since our hands were full. The other odd thing is the bank. Now when we go through the drive thru, a year later, Simon barks because not only does Shane give Amy a sucker, he also has spoiled Simon with a little bone.

As for me, I'm on my way to the grocery store, I need a recipe for a family picnic.

[THE SHORTER VERSION] *By Kathy Perry*

TOM SAWYER'S APPROACH

I decided to try a different approach this year. I decided at my age, I need lots of help keeping the grass cut. My first approach was pleading.

"Jason," I began one day, "do you think you could help your aging mother with the yard work this summer?"

When I realized guilt didn't work, I tried praise.

"You know, I'm so proud of the way you all pitch in and help me around here."

They both perked up, I knew I was getting somewhere and I was upset that I hadn't thought of that approach before.

They walked outside and got the mowers out. The little one is for trimming and the rider for the rest of the yard.

Jason filled both mowers and checked the oil.

Someone found the clippers. I went back inside the house thinking maybe this summer I would get to sit in a lawn chair while my teenagers did some of the work. As I came back outside I noticed I was standing outside holding my lawn chair, staring at two lawn mowers. Alone in the back yard!

My next approach was brute force. That did work, but the whip and chair got heavy after a few hours.

When everything else failed, I decide on the Tom Sawyer approach. Jason was the only one I managed to convince I was having fun mowing the grass. I did such a good job convincing him that when he came home last night he replied, "Mom, you know I realized mowing the lawn could be fun, so I've taken on a few odd jobs around town. I'll be mowing five different lawns this summer. Oh, by the way," as the door slammed, "can I borrow our gas can and mower?"

[THE SHORTER VERSION] *By Kathy Perry*

OUR NEW GAS GRILL

Our new gas grill was delivered last week. Being the conservative I've grown to be, naturally I assumed for the price I paid, it would come fully assembled. The only thing assembled was the box it came in.
Julie and I started working on step one at about 2:30 that afternoon. I was so excited, in spite of the fact I felt overwhelmed by two million parts spread before me. I could smell those hamburgers cooking!
Julie looked at me and laughed.
"You know, Mom, I think this is the first time I've even seen you read instructions."
I gave her a nasty look, as I wiped the sweat from my brow. I was feeling frazzled as I sorted through three different packages of unmarked assorted nuts and bolts. A few hours later, Jason wandered in and shouted. "It's beginning to look like a grill, Mom. At least the bottom half."
As I worked on into the late afternoon, I realized I was working alone. However, they both did check in from time to time. Julie kept yelling she was starving and she wanted tacos.
"Mom," Jason shouted, "you know it won't work, Mom's don't know how to put grills together."
What does he know, I thought to myself.
I looked at my watch as I tightened the last screw. It was almost 8:00. Good thing Geyer's is open all night. I pushed my hair away from my face and put my hands on my hips. I looked around to see if anyone was watching. When I realized I was alone, I pushed the button to ignite the charcoal. I stood back, but nothing happened. I wanted to cry. Jason was right!
"What's the matter Mom?" Jason shouted.
"I don't know, Do you think you can figure it out?" I pleaded.
I walked to the house and went to the basement to wash my hands when I heard Jason call me from the garage.
"Mom, come quick, watch this," he hollered.

THE SHORTER VERSION — By Kathy Perry

I couldn't believe it! My 13 year old son fixed the grill.
"How did you do it, Jason?"
"Just takes common sense, Mom." He grinned, "I turned on the gas!"

[THE SHORTER VERSION] By Kathy Perry

VACATIONS ARE WONDERFUL

Vacations, aren't they wonderful! My husband just had one. He spent every day relaxing for a few minutes. After he washed walls in the basement and the stairway, he painted the foyer. He found it necessary to scrub the kitchen floor after Simon and Amy both stepped in the paint pan he sat on the floor while he looked for another brush. Another day he spent weeding the garden, even thought it is Jasons' 4-H project. He tried so hard to keep up with the dishes and laundry.

Every day when I came home from work, he would gently suggest that I wear the same pair of shorts I'd worn the day before. I noticed when he went to the grocery for me this week, he bought several packages of paper cups and plates. He spent most of today mowing and trimming and helping me plant flowers. He had to take the dog to the vet and the kids to the pool. I heard him on the phone this afternoon talking to his boss. He's going back to work Saturday. He says they need him at the store. I can't believe he would give up his last day of vacation.

[THE SHORTER VERSION] *By Kathy Perry*

NINE TO FIVE

Just the other day my girlfriend picked up her daughter from work. Her daughter had worked three and a half hours at her new job.

The first day she came home so excited and full of joy about her new job. She came home shouting, "Mom, this job is a piece of cake."

My friend Dianne was thrilled that Beth liked her work, but wondered how long the enthusiasm would last. The second day on the job, however, was a little different. Beth found she was responsible for lots of ketchup bottles and steak sauce. Every table had salt and pepper shakers which also needed to be filled. Silverware trays and plastic serving trays needed to be washed. Tables needed to be cleared every few minutes, because "thousands" of people eat there.

After a gruesome three and a half hours, Beth called her Mom to come get her.

She fell back in the chair in the family room and kicked off her shoes. "They wanted me to work until 9, Mom, "but there was no way. I'm exhausted," as she leaned over rubbing her tired, sore feet.

She looked at Dianne with those big tired eyes.

"You know, Mom, I met a girl who's worked there for a long time; and do you know some people have to work 8 hours?"

[THE SHORTER VERSION] *By Kathy Perry*

LOTTO FEVER

Last week my family caught "lotto fever."
We finely joined the ranks along with thousands of other Americans with the "fever."
I've never bought a lottery ticket before; so I asked several friends who are weekly buyers what I needed to do.
One of them brought her tickets to work to show me what they look like, and how to fill one out. I told the kids they could help me pick numbers.
They were yelling and shouting that they knew they would pick the winning number. Jason informed me if he won $10 million he would give me $50.
Before they picked the numbers, they already knew they would win. In fact they were arguing and angry with each other for not sharing their winnings. I said, "Look, you guys, the chances of us winning are about as slim as Amy becoming a lawyer next week."
Jason thought the longest before he gave me his list of numbers. Julie just shouted out six numbers. Poor Amy thought I wanted her to count to 40.
I'm not sure how my husband selected his numbers, but I wrote them down. I put 40 numbers in a cup and drew them out; but I didn't like the first numbers I picked, so I picked some more.
Each of us confident we had picked the winning number combination, we shared our ideas on how we would spend our money.
Jason wanted to buy mini-bikes and motorcycles and lots of Civil War books.
Julie wanted to redecorate her room, including wallpaper and carpet. She also wanted to build an additional closet for all the clothes she'd buy. Amy wanted lots of gum.
My husband wanted a car.

THE SHORTER VERSION — By Kathy Perry

They all went for a long time before they asked me what I wanted. You can imagine the look on their faces when I told them.

"I think the first thing I would buy if I won $10 million would be a new, pretty collar for Simon. Then I would have my car detailed."

[THE SHORTER VERSION] *By Kathy Perry*

LOVE MOM

I've decided to rebel! When my children are grown and settled into their own homes, complete with beautiful new furniture and carpet, I'm going to visit about once a week. The first thing I'm going to do is find the biggest, prettiest towel they have and then I'm going to dry my car. After that I will untangle their 150 foot hose and leave it in the yard, along with the towel. Then I'm going to go out with the neighbor kids, play football, roll in some mud, march through the house and sit in the living room with my muddy feet propped on the coffee table. One week will be reserved for breaking a few drinking glasses. I'm going to go swimming and leave my swim suit on the dining room table, soaking wet, maybe wet enough to drip on their carpet. After I get both (the rider and the trim mower) out, just to make them think I'm going to cut the grass and trim, I'll use all the gas to ride my dirt bike all over their lawn until there is a brown path where I've ridden. I'll pour a full glass of Pepsi and leave it on the counter. I think a nice gesture would be to put the empty bottle, except for one swallow, back in the refrigerator. I'll iron my blouse and forget to turn off the iron. I think I'll do that when I first get there, so it can be on all day. The grand finale will be when I pour a full glass of milk, drink half of it, leave it on the coffee table next to the empty Oreo package, turn on the TV, unlock all the doors, and then go home. I think I'll leave a note and just sign it, "Love Mom!"

[THE SHORTER VERSION]   *By Kathy Perry*

THE COUNTY FAIR

When I was a little girl, the county fair meant different things to me. I was always in 4-H and the band, so I had to go every day.
The fair meant hurrying to finish my 4-H projects and planning the float for our 4-H club.
We always went to Mrs. Price's house to paint signs and fold streamers. I loved it. I remember the year I was also in boys 4-H and took a steer. In the morning when I woke in the steer barn, I had straw in my hair and flies on my face. I still thought the fair was great. After I rode a few of the rides I had a caramel apple, cotton candy and a few French waffles. I thought Mom was pretty mean when she made me eat dinner, after she took me home to wash my hair and take a shower. Today the fair is a different story. Even the sound of the rides moving about makes me sick. We went to the fair last weekend. Of course I had to eat cotton candy, a caramel apple and French waffles. To the list I added a funnel cake and a hot dog.
Now that it's Thursday, I should be able to eat something other than broth or 7-up.
The county fair just isn't the way it used to be.

[THE SHORTER VERSION] *By Kathy Perry*

THE GOOD STUFF

The other day I finally got tired of listening to everyone complain around here.
"No one ever cooks anymore."
"There's never anything to eat."
"Who ate the last Pop Tart?"
I told them all to file a class action law suit. Julie asked to go to the grocery store with me.
"Mom, you never buy the good stuff anymore."
I wondered what she meant by the "good stuff" so I took her with me.
Not only did I spend three times the amount I normally spend, I learned what she meant by the "good stuff."
The realization didn't hit me until I started putting the groceries away. I didn't realize how many different ways you can buy macaroni and cheese. She had boxes, bags and frozen dinners.
There were several packages of lunch meat and about ten cans of soup and Spaghetti O's.
There was enough Pepsi for an army.
Unfortunately I didn't remember half the things she bought. I distinctly remember when she asked for some pudding. I hesitated for a moment, thinking those little pre-mixed cans of pudding are always so expensive-then I nodded my approval. You can imagine the look on my face when I pulled a six pound can of tapioca pudding out of the bag.

[THE SHORTER VERSION] *By Kathy Perry*

BACK TO EARTH

There is nothing like the honesty of a five-year-old to bring you back to earth. Amy always wants to help. Most of the time she's too little.
While everyone else was picking vegetables from the garden, Amy wanted to help too. I told her to pick a few green peppers or onions. I felt either of those were "safe."
While the rest of us were in the house, chopping peppers or onions to freeze, Amy came running.
"Look Mom," she shouted as the door slammed behind her. She proudly held about 50 onions in front of her. I couldn't believe my eyes. I was sure she had picked all the onions.
"Are there any left?"
"I don't think so, Mom. Aren't you proud of me?" I smiled and nodded. Amy keeps telling me she wishes she could read, then she could help me study. Five-year-olds still like their moms. They think you are still smart and sometimes pretty.
I was in the bathroom getting dressed this morning. I reached for the hand mirror to check the back of my hair.
"You know, Mom, you look like the President."
"You mean, Nancy?" Thinking she meant my hair looked like Mrs. Reagan.
"No, not that one."
"He's the only President we have Amy."
She gave me one of those looks. "I mean the President on the one dollar bill, Mom."

[THE SHORTER VERSION] *By Kathy Perry*

NOVEMBER HARVEST

It wasn't until yesterday I realized how many flowers I have that I have to dig up every fall.

I remembered last year thinking next spring I wouldn't plant all those bulbs. As it turned out not only did I plant all those bulbs, I ordered more bulbs that also have to be dug up every fall. The worst part about it is every winter I have to water the bulbs and they multiply. So every spring I have even more bulbs.

Next year I could be in trouble though; because the way I see it, if each of us takes a turn digging up the bulbs, we can work in two hour shifts. If we start in late September we should be finished by early November. After I finished complaining to my husband about the predicament I was in he looked over the top of the newspaper.

"Well, at least we don't have all those trees to plant this year. It took a long time to plant all 100 of them. I suppose it will be nice when they have all grown."

I nodded and smiled.

"Why do you have that look on your face?" he inquired.

"Well," I thought, as I pointed, "I would really like for you to move that group of 50 trees over there and plant them over here."

[THE SHORTER VERSION] *By Kathy Perry*

THE 27 HOUR DAY

Now that school has started I'm finding that once again I'm trying to cram 27 hours into 24. If I could only figure out a way so I didn't have to sleep every day. Maybe once a week or twice a month, like a battery that needs to be recharged. Somehow I would probably plug the recharging unit into the cigarette lighter in the car while I'm on my way to a meeting, work, class, picking up or dropping off one of the kids. People have told me, as you get older, you tend to slow down. The rate I've been going I seem to have picked up momentum. Maybe I'm doing it in reverse. Some days I feel like these are my "twilight years."

I suppose starting the day at 6:30 or 7:00 and going non-stop until 12:30 or 1:00 the next morning may have something to do with it. I had all my books and notes propped around me as I sat "Indian style" on the sofa last evening, ready to study again. I didn't realize how many demands I was placing on my husband. After I'd been studying for a while, I asked him to pour a glass of Pepsi for me, then I wanted pretzels, then a cup of Suisse Mocha. After he settled back in his favorite chair with the paper, I heard him mumble, "I'm going to buy a TV with a remote control." I wonder how he knew I wanted him to change the channel.

[THE SHORTER VERSION]   *By Kathy Perry*

NOTHING TO LOOK FORWARD TO

I was sitting in the office waiting for Julie to finish a test for her driving permit when I remembered, it seemed so many years ago when I received mine. I was so nervous, knowing my life depended on whether I passed or failed my exam. My sister was just as excited for me, except for the fact that she knew after I received my drivers license, I'd have nothing to look forward to. When I look back now, I think she was right. It's been downhill ever since. After Julie got her permit, she wanted to use my car Saturday. "Mom, one of my friends has her license, she's had it for a long time, since June, I think."
"Julie, none of you has ever driven a standard gear shift before."
"Mom, really! How complicated can it be! Can't you just teach me tomorrow?"
And before I could interject my thoughts, "I've got it all figured out, Mom. On the way to work, I'll drive your car—I already know how to shift gears. I've seen you do it a thousand times. I should have it mastered in 10 or 15 minutes."
I think my sister was right—I don't have anything to look forward to!

[THE SHORTER VERSION] By Kathy Perry

NO ORDINARY DAY

I love the way my kids keep me in touch with reality. I've been so busy, with work and school, so I haven't really spent a lot of time in the kitchen. Usually Sunday, after church, I really enjoy a nice sit-down dinner. Most of the time, right after church, everyone is still speaking. During the week I usually buy hot dogs and hamburger so my husband doesn't have such a tough time trying to cook for everyone during my absence. I've been trying to prepare a few casseroles on Saturday so he can just pop them into the oven. However, he usually runs into the same snag I do. "I'm not gonna eat that stuff again, besides we just ate it last week!"

Yesterday I must have taken leave of my senses; because after I went to the store, I decided to cook. Since I didn't have to work or go to school, I felt really ambitious. I started early, baking pies and bread. The house smelled like Thanksgiving.

We had meat loaf, scalloped potatoes, corn (from the garden), homemade bread, and pumpkin pies I just removed from the oven.

It so happened that Amy and I were the only ones home to eat, but I decided not to let that dampen my spirit. I lit the candles and called Amy to the table. "Is this a holiday, Mom?"

[THE SHORTER VERSION] *By Kathy Perry*

POOR LITTLE SIMON

Only a true dog lover would appreciate my little Simon. My husband teases me all the time. "Someday I'll come home and that dog will probably be sitting in my favorite chair, reading the paper and smoking a cigar," he retorted.
Not a bad idea, I thought. Just to watch my husband come unglued the other night, I picked Simon up and told him I was going to make little angel wings and a halo for him and since I wouldn't be home on "trick or treat night" "daddy" would have to take him trick or treating this year. My husband looked at me and rolled his eyes. Poor little Simon was oblivious to the whole ordeal. "You know," he smiled, "if I would die and could come back, I'd like to be your dog."
Amy likes to get her Dad in trouble. She always tells me things she thinks I'll yell about. Yesterday morning while I was putting her hair in "piggy tails" she remarked; "You know mom, when you're not home, sometimes Dad calls Simon a dog."
My mouth dropped open and I turned Amy to face me. I leaned down and looked into those big green eyes.
"Amy, Simon is a dog."
"Gosh, Mom," she giggled, "I thought he was your little angel."

[THE SHORTER VERSION]   *By Kathy Perry*

WHAT A WEEK

In the same week I learned all my teeth may fall out and my next pair of glasses could be bifocals. My kids tell me all the time I have Alzheimer's disease. Just the other day I went to the grocery store to pick something up. I spent $47 and forgot what I went to pick up in the first place. I was in Columbus last week driving around by the airport when I realized I'd missed my turn. I was talking to my husband last night and right in mid-sentence I stopped, bewildered because I couldn't remember what I was talking about. He tried not to laugh. "You don't have a disease, you've just got a lot on your mind." What a mind, I thought to myself. That did make me feel a little better, but all my life I've been a light sleeper. I could never fall asleep with TV or the lights on. My husband says it's because I can hear the electric meter ticking. The house has to be dark and quiet. You can imagine how depressed I felt when I fell asleep in the chair. I was reading a report and writing comments on it. The pen was still in my hand and left a huge red mark on my jeans. I told the kids I dropped Jello on my lap. If the kids find out about all that happened to me this week, I'll be writing this column next week from my own little room in the nursing home.

[THE SHORTER VERSION]　　*By Kathy Perry*

MY FIRST EXPERIENCE

I thought last week was bad, losing my teeth and eyesight; but the coming week will be worse. My daughter is getting her drivers license. I've probably never appreciated my parents more than now. The other day she wanted to drive in heavy traffic. At the time I thought it would be a good experience for her. Little did I know that I was the one who would have the experience. The first thing she did was adjust the volume on the radio, after she found her favorite rock station. After we started off, she began chatting about the goings on at school that day. She seemed extremely confident as I glanced at the speedometer; I think my heart stopped for a second or so, because I think the last time I was going that fast was probably on a roller coaster. I tried not to show my alarm, but when she finally stopped the car to eat, she commented that I was a "little pale." I remember when I learned to drive. I talked my Grandmother into going with me back the lane. Dad wouldn't let me drive the car, I had to drive the truck, which had a three speed transmission. Either the truck had no shocks, or I was driving a little too fast, because poor Grandma was bouncing all over the front seat of the truck. It took me a while to get used to the clutch, too. Grandma only went with me once. When my sister learned to drive she used to take our faithful dog, Teddy. (Grandma wouldn't go.) Teddy used to brace himself by putting one foot on the seat and one on the back. My daughter tried to take Simon with her; but when he realized he was going in her car, he turned and ran back to the house.

[THE SHORTER VERSION]   *By Kathy Perry*

DON'T LET ANYTHING STOP YOU

Do you ever wonder if your kids listen to any of the infinite wisdom you try to pass on to them, or if it's as my Grandmother suggested, "you should save your breath to cool your soup."

Last week we had to take my car to the garage for minor repairs. They loaned me another car to drive home. Jason and Amy were hysterical as we pulled away from the garage. The car I normally drive is a small compact car—the loaner was an airplane, an Army tanker which probably got three feet to the gallon. I had to pull into the first gas station we passed because the gauge was below the "E" mark. Jason shouted after I put $6.00 in it. "Look Mom, that took it all the way up to the empty mark."

While we were sitting there, Jason turned to me. "What's this Mom?" One of the vents from the dash had fallen out. We stopped at the grocery store and when I tried to get back in the car I couldn't close the door. Jason got out and came around to close the door for me. We made one last stop for a pizza and when I got back to the car and tried to close the door, the handle came off in my hand. The gas peddle kept sticking, so every time I tried to accelerate we went from 10 miles an hour to about 40 miles per hour in three seconds flat. When I turned corners I always drove over the curb. I could hear poor little Amy in the back seat, first she was on one side of the car, then on the other. The first time I applied the power brakes, Amy and Jason scrambled to find their seat belts. As we were getting closer to home, I turned to Jason. "You know honey, this car is so much bigger than my car, I'm not sure it will fit in the garage."

He smiled at me, "Mom, it's just like you always tell me, when you want to do something, don't let anything stop you."

[THE SHORTER VERSION] *By Kathy Perry*

MY WINTER COAT

I've noticed my dog is getting a winter coat. I thought to myself how lucky he is, because I'm always so cold. My husband laughs because I put layers of clothes on. He claims he can always tell the season by how many layers of clothes I have on. Yesterday I had the usual amount of layers on and as I went out the door I yelled to Amy to hurry if she was coming with me. As I was backing the car out I looked in the back seat and realized Amy was wearing just a sweater. My kids must have inherited my blood, because I think I must be about three quarts low. My husband used to think I was being romantic because as soon as the temperature dropped below 70 degrees I always took blankets with me. Now he knows I'm half dead. The kids laugh when I wear a shawl over my shoulders on Sunday morning, and at night when I wrap in my favorite afghan. Just the other night as I was going through my usual routine getting ready for bed, my husband told me I really looked sexy. I almost believed him until I heard him laugh. Then I looked in the mirror.

I was wearing purple knee high socks over my red long johns. On top of that was my favorite flannel nightgown. My fuzzy pink slippers were keeping my feet warm and I'd pulled on my faithful faded pink terry cloth (I think it was a high school graduation present) bathrobe.

[THE SHORTER VERSION] *By Kathy Perry*

CHRISTMAS PAST

By this time Santa and his wife should be resting comfortably in their little house back at the North Pole. They are both probably thinking about starting their retirement. Can you imagine the job description if we had to find a new Santa for next year?

Must have management skills. Hundreds of elves will be working for you. Must be a carpenter and a doll maker, know something about trucks and trains. Must like animals, and know how to drive reindeer. Not be afraid of heights or to fly at night. Be able to smoke a pipe. Probably should lift weights in order to prepare for the heavy sack of toys you must sling over your back. Can't be afraid of fire, in case some families forget to put out the fire in the fireplace, even though the suit is flame retardant. Most important of all, you must be able to eat millions of cookies and drink gallons of hot chocolate or milk. I haven't heard that he's retiring and that's a good thing, because his boots would be pretty hard to fill.

[THE SHORTER VERSION] *By Kathy Perry*

MISTAKEN IDENTITY

If I see one more of those disgusting soap commercials! where Mom is standing next to daughter and it's up to us to tell which one is which by looking at their hands. It was probably one of those miracle births we read about in the Enquirer where Mom was 12 years old at the time she gave birth. Mom probably rubbed Oil or Olay all over the kid and herself for the past 18 years. There is so much emphasis on age today. If a man has gray hair, he has earned respect and looks distinguished. If a woman has gray hair, we all know it's been a long time between dye jobs. After 40 everything droops, even your eyelids. I always had this dream about one day walking into a store with my grown daughter and having the clerk mistake her for my sister. The other day part of my vision came true. My sister, my daughter and I were shopping and when the clerk approached us she said, "Did your sister find what she was looking for?" As I turned around, thinking she was talking to me about my sister, I realized she was talking to my sister and daughter. They both looked at me and smiled. The clerk looked at me and winked, "I know, as long as Mom pays"

[THE SHORTER VERSION] By Kathy Perry

'TIS THE SEASON'

"Tis the season. I'd like to meet the person who coined that phrase. I'll bet he or she never waited in the checkout lines at one of those "9 hour only" sales. I bet he or she didn't have to look for days to find Christmas decorations that you stuffed away last year knowing if you put them on "that" shelf you would be able to find them next year. Or after you do find all those lights, realize that "someone" took them off the tree and they are still plugged into each other, and it will probably be July before you get them untangled. I found a bag of wrapping paper and bows that Grandma wanted me to bring home and "try to use again."

I have no idea where I put the Christmas cards I ordered in July. Mom called the other day to see if I remembered where she put the lights for her tree. I got on the scales last week and I thought I heard the warning signal go off in town. I didn't get home until late the other night, and hadn't eaten since breakfast. My husband asked why I was eating dinner at 10:30.

"I'm just trying to put on a few pounds. You always told me you'd divorce me if I ever got fat and I just wondered how many more pounds I need."

[THE SHORTER VERSION] *By Kathy Perry*

POINT OF VIEW

The other day I read an interesting article. I can't remember exactly how it went, but it was about point of view. The author said if her son-in-law served her daughter breakfast in bed he was a saint, because she deserved it. However, if her son served her daughter-in-law breakfast in bed she was lazy.

I guess you've reached middle age, too, when you no longer want to wear the same outfit as your best friend. Or when you want your hair to be all the same color, that is no orange or green streaks.

There's something to be said, too, about getting into your car after one of the kids has driven it, to finds lots of McDonald's wrappers, the windshield wipers on, the radio blasting, the rearview mirror out of adjustment, the seat in several different positions and of course the gas gauge on minus empty. That's the only reason it's parked-so you can keep your fingers crossed all the way to the gas station.

It's such a joy to come home after a long day and be ale to hear my daughter's stereo as I turn the last curve on the road home. She's listening to "music" which scares me.

Guess that's just my point of view. My husband doesn't know it yet, but this weekend he's going to be a saint, and that's my Mother's point of view.

[THE SHORTER VERSION] *By Kathy Perry*

GO MOM GO

I'm noticing the older I get the less enthusiasm I have. I remember the day I got my driver's license (yes kids, it is hard to remember that far back), and a few weeks later taking the family car, and my sister, to the drive-in movie. I think we went to the drive-in every time the movie changed.
And then many years later, I remember how excited I was about becoming a mother. I couldn't wait for them to say Mama or to see them walk.
I haven't noticed much enthusiasm during the past few years, better known as the "teen" years. Maybe everything would be different if I showed a little more enthusiasm now. I'm going to run to the phone to call my mother when they pick up a dish and I think they might wash it. I'll run to load the camera when one of them acts like they are going to run the sweeper. I'll take a picture of my daughter as she shouts to me from her already moving car that she'll feed the dog when she comes home because she's already late. He only needs to eat every other day anyway.
My mother lived through two teenagers and she still has most of her sanity!

[THE SHORTER VERSION] *By Kathy Perry*

WE'RE SEXY

This was probably the happiest week of my life. While driving home from work the other day, I heard the announcer on the radio say that thin is no longer considered sexy. It's true that animals put on a few pounds in the winter. Theirs is natural around Christmas, especially if they hibernate. The announcer went on to say an extra five pounds is sexy. I must be Sophia Loren! Someone finally realized the good of hips and thighs. I thought about several of my friends who starve themselves so they can squeeze into a size 5 or 7. They go without cake or pie or chocolate covered cherries. They spend their entire life eating lo-cal dressing on their salad while sipping on a diet Pepsi. That's so boring. Life is roast beef, mashed potatoes and gravy, broccoli casserole and cherries jubilee. My closet is full of pants with elastic waistbands. I love the new dresses with the drop waist. You can hide a multitude of sin under one of those.

When I got home last night, I told Amy what I heard on the radio. After dinner I said, "Come on, Amy, let's have some hot chocolate." I told her to bring me the marshmallow cream. She looked at me reluctantly. "Mom, is it still diet hot chocolate if we put marshmallow cream in it?"

I said, "Amy, didn't you hear me? The guy said we don't have to be thin."

She smiled her toothless grin, "Does that mean we're sexy, Mom?"

[THE SHORTER VERSION] *By Kathy Perry*

EXCUSES

I sat in the recliner the other day, stuffing cookies in my mouth, wondering what my boss would say if I responded the way my children do. They all have several excuses they use every day and every once in a while they try a new one. They are always too tired to take Simon outside or to make sure he has food and water. They are too busy to do the dishes, the laundry or dust. One of them just did her nails so she can't shovel snow, another one just washed his hair, and "you don't want me to catch cold, do you Mom?" The other one, "I'm just a little kid, Mom." They all took the trash out "yesterday." They'll clean their rooms "tomorrow," because they have too much homework. When I asked them why they didn't bring their laundry downstairs, "they forgot."

They are all like my little puppy Simon, when it's time to go to the grocery store, they are waiting at the door, "because you never buy the good stuff, Mom."

When they asked me the other day if I did their laundry, I told them I was "too busy."

When they asked, "What's for dinner?" I replied, "I cooked yesterday." When they asked me to drive them to their friends house, or to the Purple Indian, I told them "I just did my nails." And the best one is when they asked when we were going to the grocery. I said "I already went, that's where I got the cookies."

[THE SHORTER VERSION]   *By Kathy Perry*

TRUST ME

My daughter always makes fun of my hair, my clothes, my shoes, my purse; but whenever I can't find one of my jackets or a purse, or my hot curlers, they are always in her room. Sometimes it takes me a little while to find what I'm looking for, because I'm never sure which chair she has filed them on, or in which order they may be. Maybe clean clothes first, then dirty clothes on the bottom or maybe vice cersa. After I found the hot curlers, I realized they weren't all there. After further investigation I discovered some of them were filed in a drawer and some of them on her bed. I found my skirt on a different chair under a carrying case for her cassette tapes. The blouse I planned to wear was on her dresser under a few albums. I decided while I was sorting through everything how I could eliminate the problem. I thought I just about had everything under control because all I needed was my jacket. I was convinced that if I would stop on the way home from work and buy a new set of hot curlers, that would eliminate one problem. Before I completely lost my temper, I found my jacket. My anger soon turned to hysteria, because as I stomped through the house with my jacket on my husband was laughing out loud.
"Now what!" I shouted, realizing I only had a few minutes before I had to leave, or be late for work.
"Do you really think you need that button on your jacket?" he replied.
I looked down at the lapel where my daughter had pinned one of her favorite buttons. It read, "Trust Me, I'm a Doctor."

[THE SHORTER VERSION] *By Kathy Perry*

SIX AGAIN

If only I could be six again. I love their logic. The other day Amy was running up and down the stairs to her room and I asked her to stop jumping off the last step. She replied, "I can't help it Mom, I'm just happy." Last week I told her she couldn't go outside to play because the chill factor was about 40 below zero. Her argument was that the sun was shinning and she didn't want to stay out long. I said okay, fine, but you're going to freeze. She put her little short jacket on and her boots and went outside. I think she barely had time to turn around before she came back inside, went quietly up to her room and changed her clothes. She's suddenly gotten weight conscious and constantly quizzes me about "fattening" foods. She wanted to know about bananas the other day, but before I could tell her she was eating the third one. She wanted to do exercises with me, so after I had been working out about 15 minutes she sat on the floor beside me, holding a cookie in each hand. "Well, come on, Amy," I shouted enthusiastically.
"Oh, I don't think so Mom" after one leg lift. She raised her tee shirt and patted her tummy, I'm already too fat."

[THE SHORTER VERSION] *By Kathy Perry*

PONY EXPRESS

Last week while driving home, I thought about how much we are inconvenienced when we have to do without something we've grown accustomed to. As I was driving through the rain which turned to slush then sleet and finally snow, I discovered half way home that I had used all the windshield solvent and it was difficult to see because of all the salt and slush the passing cars and trucks were throwing my way. I thought what it might have been like if I had been an early pioneer woman. I could envision myself driving a buckboard to work early in the morning and tying my horse to a parking meter. The thought of me driving a horse and buggy down Route 23 to Columbus did make me laugh though, because it would probably take a team of horses to get me there in an hour. Maybe I could trade ponies along the way like the Pony Express used to do. I wouldn't have to worry about hot curlers or curling irons any more. Wendy's and McDonald's would have to expand their parking lots because I usually stop on my way to school and I'm not sure I could drive a team of horses through the drive thru. I guess during those days, I wouldn't have to worry about fast food. I probably would have had to pack a lunch and dinner, too, for that matter. I wouldn't be working in town. I'd probably be in the kitchen and in the "field." I'm sure I wouldn't have been able to go to school. I might have had several more children.

At that moment my train of thought changed and I pulled into the first store to buy more windshield washer solvent and then be on my way.

[THE SHORTER VERSION] *By Kathy Perry*

NEW CAR BLUES

It's always a joy to be able to buy a new car. Just recently a friend of mine had the pleasure. For several days before, that was all she talked about. Finally when the day came for her to pick up the car, she was so excited she could hardly speak.

"Oh, Katt, won't you please go with me for a ride?" I thought it over for a few minutes, remembering her driving reputation and the fact that I'm recovering from a back injury. I looked into her hound dog eyes and decided to take a chance. The one thing that scared me more than anything was the fact that every time we stopped at a stop light, she kept thumbing through the owner's manual.

The radio was really nice except for the scan feature which she didn't know how to turn off. It automatically scanned random stations every two or three seconds, a feature I was sure my teenagers would love. She was able to make the headlights appear, but not able to turn them on.

She wanted to stop for gas because she couldn't read the gas gauge. I knew we were in trouble when she turned to me and said, "I wonder how I open the gas tank. One of these opens the hatchback, the other the gas tank. I'm going to feel pretty stupid if I pull in there for gas and I open the hatch by mistake."

[THE SHORTER VERSION] *By Kathy Perry*

SIGNS OF SPRING

I was so happy the other day when I looked outside and I saw grass. Green grass at that. I felt that we had reached a milestone. We somehow managed to survive the cold, windy winter. Finally signs of spring were arriving. My excitement was short lived however, when I came home Friday and discovered the sump pump stopped working during the "flood watch." By the time I got home the water was already working its way up the wall to the bottom step. I remember how I used to laugh at my father who would walk around with those big, ugly, black hip boots. I would have loved to have had a pair last Friday while I was standing in ice water up to my knees. My husband tends to lose his sense of humor during a crisis, maybe it was because he couldn't feel his feet anymore. Anyway, I yelled, "Guess what? Now all our friends are going to be jealous."
He looked at me like I had lost my mind. "Why?" he sarcastically replied.
I shouted back over my shoulder while running upstairs. "We have an indoor pool."

[THE SHORTER VERSION] By Kathy Perry

HO HO BREATH

My grandma used to say "people who haven't raised a family don't know what they've missed."
I'm beginning to know what she meant. It was probably not just the everyday things she was talking about. Anybody can cope with a continuous pile of laundry or stacks of dirty dishes that weren't there when you left. My daughter yelled at everyone the other day because she bought a box of Ho Ho's and only got to eat one. She shouted at me "I hate to spend all my money on food and not get to eat any of it." I tried to reason with her that I wasn't the one with the "HO HO breath." Besides I've never spent my whole pay check at the grocery store. Or maybe it's the neat little things they do, like leaving scissors on a chair for you to find later. Or a pencil left in the middle of the floor which you step on and slide half way across the room. One of the biggest thrills I've had lately was while I was using my water pik, my son casually walked into the bathroom and increased the speed of the water. I asked Amy to take the trash out the other day. Poor little Amy is the only one who doesn't yell about helping me. We had been cleaning the basement so we had several bags.
This morning when I was leaving for work, I realized how Amy was able to run back in the house so quickly. All those bags of trash were stacked neatly inside the garage, just past the entrance door, which is directly BEHIND my car.

[THE SHORTER VERSION]   *By Kathy Perry*

TOOTH FAIRY WILL KNOW

Before I had children I thought I would be one of those mothers you see in advertisements. The ones with every hair in place, beautifully manicured nails, and a nice little dress. Probably sitting in a sun filled kitchen with shiny floors, drinking tea. My daughter would be sitting across the table from me discussing a shopping trip we had just come home from. Whenever any of my children would ask a question I would calmly give them the right answer. There was never an instance I couldn't handle calmly. I don't think I ever sat sipping tea in my life. My usual attire at home is a sweat suit and my hair is always pulled up with a rubber band or combs with loose wisps hanging everywhere.

Last month I noticed Amy was trying to move one of her baby teeth. After closer examination I realized she was trying to loosen it herself, and the tooth wasn't ready to come out. I told her when a new tooth was there the new tooth would push her little baby tooth out of the way. I also mentioned the tooth fairy would know if she had pulled it out herself. Of course she didn't listen to me and after several weeks of wiggling her tooth, it finally did come out. Instead of sitting at the kitchen table calmly trying to discuss the matter with her, saying "now sweetheart, tell mother why you wanted to pull your own tooth before it was ready? " I just shouted. She yelled back that all of her friends teeth were falling out and they had been making fun of her because none of hers had fallen out yet.

I shrieked, "Amy they call you fat too, but you haven't stopped eating."

I think the tooth fairy must have had a lot on her mind that night, because she did forget to come to pick up the tooth.

The second morning Amy came running downstairs shouting, "Mom, Mom, look" she held her money so I could see "the tooth fairy did come."

She tipped her head sideways and placed her hand on her hip.

THE SHORTER VERSION — *By Kathy Perry*

"You know, Mom, the tooth fairy probably had to think it over a few days."

[THE SHORTER VERSION]   By Kathy Perry

AWAY FROM IT ALL

My kids tell me they need time to "get away." I'm not sure I understand what they mean by "getting away from it all" either. They tell me, too, that they just need a few days.

I think they mean they don't want me to do their laundry or pick up their dirty dishes from the coffee table. They probably don't want me to stay up late to take a favorite pair of jeans out of the washer at 10:30 p.m. and make sure I put them in the dryer, because they forgot to put them in the dirty clothes basket again. I think it means they don't want me to type a report at 10:30 at night, that should have been typed three weeks ago, because they have been too busy at the tanning bed and forgot all about it. They don't need me to cook breakfast or dinner, or run to the store for taco "stuff," because some friend will be dropping by for dinner. It also means they don't need my credit cards for clothes or gasoline.

They're right---motherhood is wonderful. My kids do deserve a few days "away from it all."

[THE SHORTER VERSION]   *By Kathy Perry*

LET'S GET ON THE BUS

My girlfriend had the right idea. She put her kids on a bus to her sisters' house in Virginia. She felt bad because they had to ride 9 hours on the bus. I said look at it this way Libby, you didn't have to listen to your two little "cupcakes" fighting for nine hours in the car or about which restaurant you would be eating in. So what if it takes a little longer on the bus. You didn't have to stop every 20 minutes for a potty break (there are restrooms on the bus). You also didn't have to turn around five miles down the road because your son left the dog at the last rest stop.

All the time you are driving one of them is kicking the back of your seat.

I remember once while I was driving, my son dropped a sucker behind me, then cried for half an hour because I threw it away, along with half the hair on my head it was stuck to.

My girlfriend shouldn't feel bad, because if you want to have a really good time-take your kids to the beach. As soon as Susie builds a cute little sand castle Jr. kicks it over or stomps all over it and says it was an accident. By then you decide they have both had enough sun, so you go back to the motel thinking maybe you would like to rest a little before going to dinner and a movie. After the two of them fight over who takes a shower first, you take one just so you don't have to listen to them any more. Then you try to decide on which restaurant right after another argument. Just so they don't forget how to argue, they also fight about who sleeps in which bed.

Yes, Libby had the right idea---I just bought three bus tickets to Libby's sister's house in Virginia.

[THE SHORTER VERSION] *By Kathy Perry*

PARENT ABUSE

Last week several friends of mine wanted me to meet them after work for dinner. They thought it would be fun since I didn't have to go to school all week. After we talked about everybody from work who wasn't there, we started comparing stories about our children.
Most of them have teenagers the same ages as mine, but one of them has a daughter 18 months old.
When Karen started telling us "old pros" some of the problems she was having at the grocery store, everyone had advice.
For instance Lauren would grab a bag of cookies and open them and help herself to a few when Karen wasn't looking.
Becky suggested the Dr. Spock pinch. (I never heard of it.) Another suggested handcuffs. (I hope she was joking)
When my son was that age, he used to grab all sorts of things off the shelf if I got too close. By the time I got to the check-out I would have about $200 worth of cookies and cereal in my cart. I remember one day he grabbed some fruit out of the produce section and had already taken a bite when I turned around again.
I think the most embarrassing day was when he was making me so angry I just grabbed both his arms and told him to stop. He screamed so loud, "Mom, stop you're killing me." Everyone in the check-out lanes stopped to stare at me—the unfit mother.
Well, now my son is taller and heavier than me. The other day, we were leaving the restaurant. I raised my hand and acted like I was going to slug him. He raised his arms and shouted, "Please, Mom, don't hurt me." A guy walking past us laughed and said, "I think you should hit him again."

[THE SHORTER VERSION] *By Kathy Perry*

YOU ARE A SUCCESS

My girlfriend Mavis called the other day in tears. Without hesitation, I sighed, I know Mavis, you don't have to say anything. I have teenagers too."

She finally blew her nose. "You know, I really think I must be a terrible parent." She started crying again. I interrupted her. "You just have to understand teenagers. They wash one pair of jeans at a time. They ask to drive your car when theirs is out of gas. They kiss the dog on the lips, but refuse to drink after their sister. They look at you like you are brain dead when you ask them to wash dishes, help with the laundry, clean their room, or cut the grass. The only time they say a kind word to you is when it involves money. You are imagining things when you can't sleep at night because they aren't home yet."

Mavis let out a little sigh. "The only thing I've ever wanted," she said, "was for them to be happy. I've always felt that is how I would know I was a successful parent."

"Look at it this way, Mavis." After your children are grown and you are still coherent enough to be able to tie your shoes, then you've been a success."

[THE SHORTER VERSION] *By Kathy Perry*

SUMMER COLDS

Have you ever noticed that when you have a sore throat or a cold or even the flu, everyone becomes a doctor. For the past two weeks I've had bronchitis and an upper respiratory infection. After two trips to the doctor and two weeks of "sleeping" I still didn't feel much better.

People began calling saying, "I saw on TV the other day if you get a summer cold you should sit in the sun."

Another friend said, "MY uncle had a cold like that and he took a whole bottle of those little vitamin C tablets."

And still another well meaning friend suggested I drink hot tea with honey and lemon.

Of course during the entire time my children were constantly asking if they could do anything around the house to help. Actually I don't think any of them realized I was sick. After several weeks of not feeling any better, I decided to take my friends advice.

I started taking vitamin C on Friday morning. On Saturday morning I drank hot tea with honey and lemon and then I sat outside in the sun.

When I realized, several hours later that I was pretty pink, it was too late. Because on Sunday morning I looked like a swollen, refried bean with a summer cold.

[THE SHORTER VERSION] *By Kathy Perry*

VISIONS

If I had known many years ago that when my children were teenagers, it would be "preppy" to walk around with their shoes untied, I never would have spent so much time trying to teach them how to tie their shoes.

I remember all the times in the grocery store when my son would be sitting in the cart and every time I got too close to anything he would grab it and put it in the cart. I used to grab his arms (when I could catch him) and tell him to stop. I'd say now stop or I'm gong to break your arm. He would only retaliate by shouting "You stop-you're killing me." In the middle of the store other mothers gathered giving me the most disgusted look.

The other day my son went with me to visit a dear friend of ours who was just admitted to a nursing home. As we were walking through the lobby to leave, which was filled with senior citizens and their friends or family, my son did it to me again. He reached down and put his arm around my shoulders and said in his loudest voice, "I'm so glad you're finally getting out of here, Mom."

[THE SHORTER VERSION] *By Kathy Perry*

FAMILY VACATIONS

While driving home Friday night I noticed a station wagon ahead of me, which was loaded down with luggage. Dad was puffing a cigar, Mom was reading a road map, and it looked like Junior and his sister were fighting in the backseat.
As I was driving along I was reminded of some of the family vacations we have taken.
One summer we went to Cedar Point and after we had been there several hours they were bored. I remember shouting "how in the world could anyone be bored at Cedar Point." What they really meant was they didn't like waiting in the long lines. And I think they were starting to feel sick from all the junk food they had already inhaled. One summer they said, "Mom, you never take us anyplace." So I packed the car and took them to Florida. They sat in the backseat and fought about which restaurant we would eat in. They fought about who would fall asleep first in the back seat. They kicked the back of my seat as I drove. They fought about who would get in the car first, and who would get out of the car first. When we got to Florida they fought about who would sleep in which bed. They fought about who would swim in the pool first and who would get back to the room first. I remember I didn't get a lot of sleep while we were there, so I was really anxious to go back home. When I finally got the car all packed and everybody in it, they fell asleep. I woke them once when we were in Georgia to eat. After we ate they fell back asleep. We were half way through Kentucky by the time I made up my mind I could make it the rest of the way home. I remember Julie woke up, rubbed her eyes and said, "Are you still awake, Mom?"

[THE SHORTER VERSION] By Kathy Perry

FIFTY DOLLARS AN HOUR

Last week I thought I'd hit pay dirt. No, not the lottery. My son spent three hours cleaning his room. After about 100 trips up and down the stairs with garbage bags, I finally got the courage to ask, "Is there anything left in your room?"

"Of course," he shouted over his shoulder. "Come upstairs and see for yourself."

For years I've always warned friends and family alike not to go near the upstairs of my house unless they have recently had a tetanus shot. After he burned the last bag of trash and packed all the clothes he could no longer wear, he finally persuaded me to follow him upstairs. As I turned to walk into his room, I realized there weren't any weights to step over in the doorway. There were no dirty clothes on the floor. I noticed he actually had nice carpet. It had been years since I had seen it. He even had a nice bedspread which still matched the carpet. I was overwhelmed. Like a child at Cedar Point for the first time.

I turned to give him a big hug. "I'm so proud of you honey, and it only took three years for you to do this. You've done such a good job on your room, why don't you clean your sisters room. I'll pay you." I added.

He looked at me like I was brain dead. "Here are the terms, Mom. Fifty dollars an hour and you have to rent a dumpster to sit below her window."

[THE SHORTER VERSION]   *By Kathy Perry*

ALL IN A NAME

A few weeks ago, while I was still recovering from bronchitis, I got hooked on afternoon soaps. I couldn't believe some of the names of the characters. I watched a show the other day, the guy's name was String. Then there is Fallon, Crystal and Blake. How about his ex-wife Alexis? Can you imagine a family reunion where Uncle Joe brought pictures of his children, Sloan and Jordy and their children Roxy, Zed and Mason? Or Aunt Lulu's daughter, Channing (or was that her son), or the twins Cruz and Caliope?

I could really identify with some of the women on those shows. Does anybody ever work? The doctors and nurses are always talking. The wives and girlfriends are at "benefit luncheons." And you never know whose husband is with whose wife. I wonder who buys the groceries? Their children are babies one day and three months later they are a doctor or a politician.

I think tomorrow I'll sleep in until 9:00 and then have my nails and hair done, before I meet Caliope for a "benefit luncheon."

[THE SHORTER VERSION] *By Kathy Perry*

I'M MOVING

When I was a little girl I remember how much fun holidays and weekends were. All that good food and no school. Today weekends and holidays mean getting up early to start cooking, catching up on the laundry, and cleaning the house. Cooking for people I've never seen before. Don't you just love it when your son comes home with two or three buddies who could devour half a cow by themselves? By the time you cook a bigger breakfast than during the week, finish the dishes, clean up the kitchen it's time to start lunch. Of course everyone offers to help. They shove their plates to the middle of the table, then either lay in front of the TV or swim until it's time to eat again.

After lunch when a nap sounds wonderful, everyone else has the same idea. So there's no available couch space. A very dear friend of mine is now a resident of East Lawn Manor. Most days she feels sad because she's there. I tried to help her look on the bright side. She doesn't have to cook, do the dishes, wash or iron clothes and she gets her hair done on Tuesday.

I think I'll buy some change of address cards. I could be her roommate. My son says I could pass for "90" any day.

[THE SHORTER VERSION] *By Kathy Perry*

WE'RE GOING HOME

Ever notice, if you can remember, the older you get the worse your memory is. I probably only have a few years left. I can't remember anything anymore. I've always been so organized. One day I made whipped topping. I put the mixer in the refrigerator and the whipped topping back in the cupboard. While putting the groceries away and talking on the phone at the same time, I piled the pantyhose right next to the soup. I've walked to the kitchen just to stand there because I can't remember why I'm even in the kitchen. I walk up and down the aisle at the grocery store and pick up everything but the one or two things I came for. I paid a bill the other day and forgot where I stuck it. As I was checking the appointment book, I carry in my purse, the check fell out on the floor. We stopped at the post office the other day, and when I got back in the car, I turned to my son and said, "I forgot where we are going now."

He looked at me like I had just asked him to clean his room, "We're going home, Mom."

[THE SHORTER VERSION] *By Kathy Perry*

ONE LESS TOOTH

For the past two weeks I've been trying to cook things Amy could eat minus a tooth. When her second tooth got loose, she had a terrible time trying to eat anything. One morning she was trying to eat cereal and every time she closed her mouth, the loose tooth would slide down on her bottom teeth and cause a lot of pain. I tried to reassure her that maybe it would fall out that day. I think I was as disappointed as she when she came home with that tooth still hanging from her gum. I thought she might be able to swallow meatloaf and mashed potatoes. While we were in the kitchen she wanted me to try again to pull the tooth. The first time it didn't come out, but the second time it did. She was thrilled to death. A few nights later, the two of us were alone for dinner, so we decided pizza sounded good. While we drank our pop waiting for the pizza, she talked about school and all her friends who had lost teeth. As we sat eating the pizza, she smiled and said, "You know, Mom, my gums can eat this pizza pretty good."

[THE SHORTER VERSION] *By Kathy Perry*

DAD'S COOKING

The other day I asked my husband to help because I had so many things to do that morning before I left for work. Being the optimist that he is he volunteered freely. "What would you like me to do?" he asked. "Well, could you make some Cream of Wheat?" He stared at me for a second, then turned around and marched into the kitchen.

Amy and I don't like it with salt in it, but I forgot to tell him. When Amy took the first bite I knew something was wrong. So I tried to tell him tactfully that we don't like the salty taste. Over the weekend he made Jello and a few days later he offered to make cream of wheat for us again.

Amy and I were in the bathroom where we always have our "girl talks." She said, "I'm so glad Dad finally learned how to make Cream of Wheat, Mom." I laughed, "better wait until you taste it, Amy. Oh, you're probably right," I continued "how can you mess up Cream of Wheat?"

She stepped back in the bathroom, and whispered, "I don't know, Mom, how could he mess up Jello?"

[THE SHORTER VERSION]   By Kathy Perry

FOR THE LOVE OF SIMON

My column is a little different this week, because I have a broken heart.

Due to a remodeling project and a door that was opened, my little Simon was able to get outside and on to the road. A kind person saw little Simon lying alongside the road after he had been hit, picked him up and put him in a box by my house.

My son buried little Simon under a tree for me before I got home from work.

I see Simon everywhere. When I sit in the dining room, he isn't beside my chair so I can pretend I'm not feeding him from the table. I don't have to scoot over on the sofa for him to sleep beside me anymore.

He's not there in the middle of the night to be angry with me for taking up too much space in bed.

I will never see his little floppy ears as he ran down the hill to catch up with me on the lawn mower. He will never ride with me while I'm cutting the grass.

He is gone for now, but I will never forget that adorable little guy.

Only another dog lover will understand how much I miss little Simon. He wasn't "just a dog," he was part of my family.

[THE SHORTER VERSION]　　*By Kathy Perry*

CAREFUL SHOPPER

My kids laugh at me all the time because they say I'm cheap. I prefer to think I'm a careful shopper. My kids say it's not normal to get excited because laundry soap is on sale. They make fun of me, too, because I buy several cans of things at one time. Especially if the price is right. One night I came home with three grocery bags full. My husband came to the door to help me with my "heavy" load. You should have seen the look on his face when he realized it was all toilet paper. They laugh at me because I cut out coupons. The only time they don't laugh is when I get money back. I never want to run out of lemonade. I almost always buy a can when I stop at the store. However, one night I realized I would have to stop buying it for a while because we had six or seven cans of the frozen stuff.

I always try to make sure the oldest can is used first, but I'm not the only one who opens the cans. The other night my son opened a can and found a coupon on top. He laughed when he handed it to me, but that's not unusual. I realized why he was laughing when I looked at the coupon. The expiration date was 12-23-83—two years old.

[THE SHORTER VERSION] *By Kathy Perry*

I'LL TOUCH YOUR TRAP

My son mentioned the other day that he wanted to hunt and trap. Imagine my concern when I came home and he appeared to be "cooking" his traps in black, waxy water on my stove. When I yelled at him to get out of my kitchen with his nasty mess, he informed me it was necessary to dye and wax them before he could use them. I opened the freezer, thinking I would find something for dinner. I saw a sack I hadn't seen before. As I started to open it, I heard my son running and yelling. "Don't open that bag, Mom."
"What's in there?" I questioned.
"Mom, believe me, you don't want to know."
I felt he was probably right, but I pursued the matter.
"Well, Mom," he continued, "if you must know, it's spoiled meat."
I think I screamed, "Why is it in the freezer now?"
He bought boots and a shovel. He also said he needed a pair of gloves because he didn't want to get his scent on the traps after he dipped them.
This little hobby that he claims is going to make him rich, has cost me a fortune.
Now I do have an edge on him. When I tell him to take out the trash and he says he's busy, I just tell him, "Fine, I'll go touch your traps."

[THE SHORTER VERSION] *By Kathy Perry*

KOKO'S HOME

I thought the days, well really the nights of getting up with babies was over forever. My children thought I needed a puppy to help me get over losing Simon. I wasn't happy about the idea at first. My heart is still hurting.
Well, they brought KoKo home, and he is so adorable. He is a deep rich, chocolate brown long hair miniature Dachshund. Just like Simon, only brown.
We've only had him two days and so far we have taken about six rolls of film. He has logged about 400 miles in the car, because all my friends and relatives had to see him. He's already made his first trip to the vet, and we made sure Sandi wrote his birthday down because next year we expect a little birthday card. The only thing he hasn't done so far is sleep---at night, that is. As long as I carry him, sit with him on the sofa or take him in the car, he sleeps like a baby. When I go to bed I put him in his bed which is in the kitchen. He's so tiny I thought I could sneak him into my bed and my husband would never know because he sleeps so sound.
If KoKo was housebroken, my husband would never have known.

[THE SHORTER VERSION] *By Kathy Perry*

HE'S A TAILGATE

If I have to spend one more Sunday afternoon watching football I think I'll be sick. I do enjoy listening to my husband scream when the other team is winning. He actually jumps out of the chair and screams. He always gets upset if I'm not in the same room with him. I enjoy reading a book in another room where it's quiet. I don't enjoy watching a bunch of grown men run with a little ball down the field. They keep running into each other, falling in a pile, then eventually limping off to the sidelines. Maybe if I knew more about the game I would enjoy it. I'm not the only woman who doesn't understand or should I say want to understand football. The other day at work one of the girls complained about the same thing. She said, "You know, I'm really tired of being a football widow. When my son first started playing football, I tried to act interested. I asked him what position he was playing. When my husband came home I thought he would be impressed with my new knowledge of football. Guess what position Brad is playing," my girlfriend stated, "it's either a nickelback or tailgate."

[THE SHORTER VERSION] *By Kathy Perry*

WE HAVE RIGHTS

I think it's time we parents take a stand. You know, parents have rights too. Not many, but we do have rights. We have the right to shop for groceries. We have the right to bring them home and put them away where ever we want. We have the right to cook meals, so the kids can say, "What is this stuff?" or "I'm not eating this-you know I hate turkey, dressing and mashed potatoes."

We have the right to clean the house in the morning, so that by the time you go to bed it looks like the house blew up-again. We have the right to do the laundry, several times a day. When you open the closet and there is an empty basket you feel great until someone says, "Mom, have you washed jeans yet? I'll get mine from my room."

We have the right to give them our last $10 for a tape, because if we need more money, we can just write a check. It doesn't really matter, because I know my kids appreciate everything I do.

Oh, we also have the right to put gas in the car so "they" can drive it all out and bring it home!

[THE SHORTER VERSION] *By Kathy Perry*

TRAPPER JOHN

I NEVER DREAMED "trapper John" would love "fish stories." It's incredible the creatures he has caught in his trap already. So far everything has "gotten away."

It amazes me how my child can get up before daylight, walk in the rain for over an hour, recognize all the tracks around his trap, but not notice he has mud on his boots as he walks thru the kitchen. It's incredible, all the little creatures he has spotted. A deer, a possum, a rabbit, a fox (red) and a skunk. He feeds them every day. He tells me he's not "feeding" them, he's baiting the trap. All the little animals show up during the night for their little snack. He asked me the other day if it would be OK to put a fox or whatever he caught in the freezer to preserve the fur. I told him if I opened the freezer and found anything but cow, he would have to live in a tent.

If he is this ambitious when he starts fishing in the spring, I'm sure a 20 pound tuna will snap his line at the State Lakes.

[THE SHORTER VERSION] *By Kathy Perry*

PEARLS OF WISDOM

I think I understand why my children don't always accept the pearls of wisdom which flow from my lips. The other night my son ran around the side of the house to surprise my husband with snowballs. My husband was trying to carry Christmas presents into the house. My husband very carefully put the packages back into the car and started chasing my son. It had been years since I had been in a snowball fight, so I untied the dog and told him he was on my side. The moon was full that night, so I had no trouble seeing. I packed several snowballs and started running behind the house. I was about two feet from my son when I slipped on a piece of paneling which was snow-covered. I scared my son so badly, it was worth it just to see the surprised look on his face. I think he screamed like a girl. When we came back into the house I thought hot chocolate sounded great. All the mugs were in the dishwasher. Just recently it has started leaking, so the minute the rinse cycle is finished, I disconnect it from the sink and push it back to it's spot beside the cupboard. I think I must have been in a hurry, because when I disconnected it and I was trying to shove the hose into the little compartment, it started the final rinse cycle. I looked like I had just stepped from the shower. No wonder my family thinks I have such infinite wisdom.

[THE SHORTER VERSION] By Kathy Perry

M.A.T.

Every time I pick up a newspaper, I read about different organizations and they all have initials. After I read through the article, I usually forget what the initials stand for and I usually reread the article two or three times. Who would guess SDI is Strategic Defense Initiative or that OMB is Office of Management and Budget? I've decided to start my own organization. It's going to be called MAT or Mothers Against Teens. I'm going to have a system installed in my house where an alarm goes off and four steel walls drop around the person who leaves the cap off the toothpaste. Those same four walls will fall around the person who turns the TV on and then leaves the house. The other punishment I've decided on is to make them be seen with each other in public places at noon. If I'm really upset with them that day, I might make them talk to each other. Whenever anyone eats or drinks anything anywhere in the entire house and they don't put the dishes in the dishwasher after they rinse them, the dish or glass will automatically be glued to their body for one week. Anyone who leaves wet towels on the floor or the dining room table, will only be allowed to use a wash cloth as a towel for three days.
I may not be the Mother of the Year-again, but this year I don't care because I have my own club!

[THE SHORTER VERSION] *By Kathy Perry*

PERMANENT VACATION

The only thing bad about vacations is the fact that they can't last longer. I suppose it wouldn't be a vacation if it lasted longer than a week or two. Besides that, it took almost a month to get ready to go and it took almost a week to get over it. I didn't have to cook or clean up, do laundry or buy groceries. I did have to stay awake. I'm used to going to bed by 10 p.m. My husband thinks I've watched too many movies, because the whole time we were away, I could envision the largest party Morrow County ever had---at my house. Whenever I called home my daughter assured me that all was well. I didn't get really nervous until I got home and realized the sweeper had been run (it was still sitting in the dining room) and the entire house had been dusted. (Probably for fingerprints.)

Every day, I stayed in bed until I felt like getting up. I ate breakfast, lunch and dinner when I felt like it. I laid on the beach or by the pool. When I wasn't asleep, resting or eating, I went shopping. Yes, vacations are always too short. However, I think I'll call my new best friend and see if she'll give me a loan so I can always be on vacation. I can't remember my new best friend's name, but she works at the bank.

[THE SHORTER VERSION] By Kathy Perry

THE MOUTHS OF BABES

I remember when I was little, my Grandmother used to laugh about a program Art Link-letter used to have. Grandma used to laugh abut the funny things her children, her grandchildren and later even her great-grandchildren used to say. When I remember the funny things even my kids say, I could write a book. In a restaurant one day my daughter wanted a grilled cheese sandwich, but my son thought she was saying "girl" cheese, so he ordered a "boy" cheese sandwich.

He thought bicentennial quarters were "bicentennial" quarters.

As far as I'm concerned, they both still "talk" funny. Now all they talk about is cars, clothes and traps. Poor Amy. I thought she was okay, now that she's in school. She used to love "bussgetti."

The other day we were going shopping and as we were driving we had to wait for a train. Amy was sitting in the front seat with me, talking nonstop as she usually does. I was concentrating on something else when I realized Amy was asking me a question. At the same time, I noticed the caboose and I started the car again. Amy looked at me and smiled, excited that we would soon be on our way again. "Look, Mom," she shouted. "There's the "commode."

[THE SHORTER VERSION] *By Kathy Perry*

THEIR DAY IS COMING

My children told me the other day that living here is worse than living in a prison. In fact, my son calls me 'warden' on a regular basis.

He tells me on a weekly basis life would be easier in prison, or a concentration camp. He compares my cooking with 'C-rations'. About once a month he tells me he's going to join the Air Force. I keep sending his name in for free literature, but so far he hasn't taken the hint. I've been trying to enlist myself, but they won't take overweight, gray haired women. I keep telling them, I only need to enlist until my teenagers are in their 20's or until I'm no longer brain dead. A friend of mine told me several months ago how wonderful her teenage daughter was. She said she was a "joy" to be around. I was recently surprised when that same mother was checking out boarding schools in China. It seems her "joy" has her driving permit and now calls her mother everyday at work trying to "borrow" her car. Her boyfriend has a drivers license and can go with her. Well, I've said it before, parents of teenagers, don't despair, someday our children will grow up. They will get married and have children. And those children will someday be teenagers.

[THE SHORTER VERSION] *By Kathy Perry*

IT'S ALIVE

The other night my husband and I were watching the news when the electric went off. Since it was late, we decided we might as well go to bed. We have a waterbed, so I hoped the electric wouldn't stay off too long or I could wake up like a Popsicle. I don't know why, but whenever anything happens that affects our waterbed, it's always in the winter. I think we might have to buy a bed for all seasons. One that we won't get frostbitten if the electric goes off. I worried about the clock, because without electricity, I was afraid I wouldn't wake up in time for work. Since the phone is cordless and also electric, we had no phone except for the one in my daughters room. I told one of my friends at work about my night. She said, "Why didn't you use your daughter's phone and call me? I would have called you in the morning."

I shouted, "You want me to go upstairs after dark? I have been in my daughters room before when the phone started ringing, and I couldn't find the phone with the light on. It's easier to run downstairs and answer the phone. Another friend confided that she's so embarrassed when people come over because all the bedrooms are on one floor. She said her daughter has two dining room chairs in her room. I told her the only advice I could offer is to take a scoop shovel and move everything away from the door—then close the door and hang a quarantine sign on the closed door. That might keep guests from mistaking the closed door for a bathroom. My dear friend Annelle said, "I think I'm beginning to understand why kids are afraid to turn the light off at night---something could be alive in there!"

[THE SHORTER VERSION]   *By Kathy Perry*

LINDA'S LUCK

Last week some friends and I had a ten year reunion of sorts. Linda, Joan and Rhonda met me for dinner one night. Even though we promised we would all keep in touch when I left, somehow we managed to let those years slide by.

Linda and Rhonda are both "Mom's" now, and most of the evening Joan and I were crying from laughter. Linda used to come to work looking like Miss America. Her long nails were beautifully manicured, her hair just so, and her clothes-I almost forgot-she wore a different outfit every day—from earrings to purse and shoes. The thing about Linda though, she had a new crisis everyday. I loved her then and I love her now, but whenever she tells me one of her stories I laugh so hard my face hurts. The bad thing is her stories aren't supposed to be funny. She told us about the night she was upset with her husband because he left to watch a wrestling match and her children were at her mothers. Because she was bored she decided to wash her hair. Just as she had lots of suds the electric went off. She managed to feel her way downstairs and was able to finally locate a lantern her husband had received for Christmas. Since he had never used it she had to put the oil in it. She spilled the oil all over the tablecloth, which was vinyl. When she tried to light the lantern the tablecloth ignited. The contorted look on her face as she described the melted tablecloth made us feel as though we were there. As she looked for something to put the fire out someone was knocking on the door. She ran to see who it was, thinking it might be someone who could help, and found two little boys asking to borrow candles. We told her she should have given them the table. We've decided to meet every month. We can't wait for Linda's next crisis. She told us that night she would never leave her husband. We all smiled at her, thinking "young love." Linda smiled. "I like my mother-in-law too much!

[THE SHORTER VERSION] *By Kathy Perry*

TURN THE WATER OFF, JOAN

My husband always gets upset with me because I don't read the instructions. That's probably one of the reasons Joan and I get along so well. She reminded me the other day of an incident years ago. I had completely forgotten about and it was one even I failed to mention to my husband. Joan told me her girlfriend came over one night to help her do some plumbing work. She said "The little thing in the back of the toilet quit working, so we went to the store to find a replacement."

She told me the instructions were simple enough- "Just take one bulb off and replace it with the new one. Put the cover back on the tank- and you're in business!

Well, according to Joan, the instructions didn't say to unscrew the bulb, so she pulled it off. Then she couldn't get the new one to stay on and without the bulb on the little arm she couldn't get the water to stop running.

Many years ago she didn't have any water in the sink and she had been brushing her teeth in the bathtub. So one night we decided to try to fix it. I told her to turn off the water. She yelled back up stairs to me that she had turned off the water and it was OK for me to start working. Well, with the second turn of the pipe wrench, water started shooting everywhere—of course it was hot water. It hit me in the face and my clothes were completely saturated in a matter of seconds. I ran to the basement with the pipe wrench, thinking we had broken the main water line. As I ran thru the laundry room, Joan was leaning up again the dryer looking at her nails.

"What's wrong? Why are you all wet?"

I shouted, breathless by now, "hurry, help me, where is the main water line-we've got big problems!" She pointed- I just turned it off. She was pointing behind the washer---she had ONLY turned the water off behind the washer!

[THE SHORTER VERSION] By Kathy Perry

DOUBLE TIME

This has been one of those "double time" weeks. You know, after you're sick a few days you have "double" laundry, "double" housework and not a thing in the house to eat. My poor children have been so hungry for almost a week. We've been out of Twinkies and HoHo's all week. My son has become weak. He's so weak it took him a half hour to wind up the hose for me after I washed my car. I know it wasn't fair of me to drag him away from the TV set on a Saturday afternoon. He had movies to watch. He said I was being unreasonable when I asked him to help me plant some flowers. When I got most of the yard work finished, I came back inside to find the dishes still sitting on the counter, waiting to be washed. I asked my son to do the dishes, but he had too much homework. I asked him to bring a basket of clean clothes upstairs and put more clothes in the washer. He said he would "after while." I felt like a failure as a mother. None of my kids ever listen to me. After asking my son for the fiftieth time to wash the dishes, I decided to blackmail him. I said, Sweetheart, if you don't do the dishes right now, I'm going to tell all your friends you like to plant petunias."

[THE SHORTER VERSION] *By Kathy Perry*

IT'S CHICKEN

My son would have been happier if he had been born 100 years ago. He thinks it would be great to "catch" dinner. When he leaves the house to shoot groundhogs, I sense he thinks he'll be face to face with Moammar Khadafy. When I ask him why he "needs" all that he takes with him, he just tells me he will "bring" home dinner. When he was little, I took him fishing once. I don't really know what it was we caught, but they were only a couple inches long. I remember how he told me several of them "fought."

I thought he should be able to brag about the fish he caught. So we cooked the fish. It was the first (I might add only) time I ever caught or cooked fresh fish. It wasn't until my son started eating the fish that I noticed little "scales" on his lips. That was the last time I ever went fishing with my son. Maybe that one experience is one of the reasons my son doesn't value my opinion when it comes to fishing or hunting. I can't wait to see the look on his face when he learns what we're having for dinner. I think I'll tell him it's "chicken."

[THE SHORTER VERSION] *By Kathy Perry*

IT'S OUR TREAT MOM

I had a dream the other night. Actually, it was more like a nightmare. I dreamed my kids borrowed my car and when they returned it, it had a full tank of gas and they washed it. The radio was on the same station I left it on, the seat in the same position and the mirrors were the way I left them.

I came home, there were no school books on the dining room table, or sweaters and jackets on the backs of the dining room chairs. The TV, stereo, radio, curling irons and iron were all turned off. I opened the linen closet and all the laundry was gone. I opened the washer and there was a full load of clothes (not just a pair of jeans). The dryer was full of clothes, too. I couldn't believe my eyes, so I walked upstairs. I opened the refrigerator. There was a full bottle of Pepsi with the lid on. The milk on the shelf beside it (not on the counter). I opened the jar of peanut butter and there wasn't a drop of jelly in the jar. The potato chip bag was rolled up and the box of Twinkies still had four in it.

All my clothes were in my closet, not on my daughter's chair or worse yet, on her floor.

I knew I was dreaming when the three of them appeared before me and said, "Mom, let us take you out for dinner-our treat!"

[THE SHORTER VERSION] *By Kathy Perry*

HAPPY BIRTHDAY TO ME

I decided this year instead of waiting for my kids to forget my birthday I would do myself a favor. So I called Bonnie. She said, "It's your birthday, huh? Well, come on over, I'll do your hair after Kim gives you a facial and a manicure."
Well, it was pure heaven. For two hours those two just pampered me. Kim painted a tiny daisy on my pinky. It was so great I decided to celebrate something every month. As it turned out, nobody forgot (maybe it was because of my hair and manicure). Lots of friends sent me cards. They even baked a cake. One brave friend had a sign staked in my front yard. In fact, I was feeling pretty good about the whole day. My Mom cooked all my favorites. But Amy brought me back to reality. Sometimes my children make me appreciate Planned Parenthood. Anyway, Amy in her innocence mentioned a song she had heard at school. She sang some of the lyrics to me. I said, "Amy I know that song, Would you like me to sing it to you? She nodded and smiled. Thinking she was enjoying the song, I remembered from high school, I said, "What are you thinking, Amy?" "That's really neat, Mom. Is that song from the olden days?"

[THE SHORTER VERSION] *By Kathy Perry*

GRANDPARENTING

The other day I talked to a friend of mine who has lots of grandchildren. I asked if her life was calmer now that she was a grandparent. She said, "Are you kidding?" Now I have more people who need me. I'm on the road all the time. If it isn't one of my kids, then it's one of their kids."

I've been depressed ever since. I realized when each of my children is married, I'll have three more children. If each of them has three children, I'll have nine grandchildren and I don't have the energy to think about great-grandchildren. I feel like I'm shifting gears in a car; I'm in second gear now. I have so much "fuel" for my grandchildren. Those little babies will love coming to Grandma's because I'm going to leave their parent's room just as it is. That way I won't have to say do you know how your mom, or your dad, used to keep their room; I can show them! I'm keeping notebooks on each of my children from the day they were born until they move out. On the day they move, I'm going to lock that book in a bank vault, because someday I'm sure I'll need the "evidence."

Several days before graduation, Amy knew I was upset. She tried to do little things to cheer me up. She picked flowers one day, arranged them in a vase and set it on the dining room table. Another day she read me a story. We were shopping the other night for a graduation dress, and when her sister came out for me to see the dress, I had a big lump in my throat. Amy took my hand "Are you gonna cry already, Mom?" I shook my head no. "Just think, Mom," Amy beamed still trying to cheer me up. "It won't be any time at all before you'll have to write about me too."

[THE SHORTER VERSION] *By Kathy Perry*

MA MA'S REVENGE

I can't believe my sweet little dog KoKo. He loves my daughters cat. The cat-the pregnant cat- rests peacefully in the morning sun, with the tip of her tail twitching. Little KoKo licks her head then rests his tiny head on her extended stomach. As she cleans her paws in the morning KoKo sneaks over by her hoping for one loving lick from MaMa cat. I'm wondering how KoKo will react when MaMa has her babies. He follows her all over the house. If she falls asleep on the footstool KoKo jumps up there beside her. Sometimes she hides on the chair in the dining room, just to free herself from the little Cassanova. He doesn't seem to mind if she has a few bites of his puppy chow, although she won't share her Meow Mix. When KoKo is outside doing what dogs do outside, MaMa sits in the window watching her "charge." Sometimes KoKo takes his ball to MaMa hoping she will play with him. MaMa is "due" to have her babies any day and I noticed the other day she seemed irritated with KoKo.

I've always thought dogs were by far the intelligent animal. MaMa cat hobbled upstairs, and of course KoKo followed her. As soon as KoKo was upstairs Mama cat came back downstairs and stretched out on the dining room floor in the morning sun. KoKo has always been afraid to come back downstairs. So in this case who is more intelligent?

[THE SHORTER VERSION] *By Kathy Perry*

SUNDAY MORNING QUEST

Sunday morning used to be such a joy. When the kids were little it was so simple. All I had to do was cook breakfast and feed it to them. After I dressed them I put them in the playpen while I got dressed for church. Now Sunday mornings are no longer a mission-they are a quest.

I have to convince my teenaged children why they want to go to church with us. The problem is not waking Amy to go, but the fact that she doesn't have two or three hours to play before time to go. After I help her get dressed I have to convince her to sit quietly while I herd everyone else in and out of the bathroom. My son has to take a shower before he does anything-before he mows the lawn, before he cleans his room, before he helps me fold clothes. It's funny, because three years ago he was the same kid with moss growing from his toothbrush. Just recently I've had a change of heart, because now all I have to do is tell Casey, the dog, to help me wake everybody for church. She runs to my son's room first to find a sock, then she jumps on his bed and tries to bark with the sock in her mouth. It's the funniest sound I've heard for a while. As I follow her from room to room watching her awaken everyone on her special mission, I usually have tears in my eyes from the laughter. Everyone comes downstairs trying to find Casey-to choke her for waking them.

But Casey is sitting quietly at my side while I drink my tea. Casey looks at me like we have a special secret and she knows they can't touch her!

THE SHORTER VERSION — By Kathy Perry

ONE MORE?

My husband mentioned, to deaf ears I might add, that he would like to have another child. I told him just the other day, I read that men may be able to do that now. I said, if you want another child, go ahead and have one-I'll even go through Lamaze with you."

He may have changed his mind last weekend. It's been a long time since we've had any small children around.

My girlfriend called and she couldn't find anyone to watch her two children. I had worked half the day and when I came home I planned to paint the kitchen. I had most of the doors off the cupboards and had everything in the middle of the kitchen floor when she called. Her little boy is three years old, her little girl is 18 months. Little David had a battery powered car he was riding in all around the yard, so my husband was outside watching him.

Tiffany was in the kitchen with me. She was sitting quietly on the floor petting Casey, who kept giving her affectionate licks and Tiffany giggled. Casey likes to sit and eat, so Tiffany walked over and picked up hands full of dog food for Casey, who was loving the extra attention. I thought all was well, even though Tiffany occasionally splashed water out of the dog's water dish. So I decided to start painting the cupboard doors again. I laid them on a sawhorse to dry and Tiffany came over to play patty-cake on my freshly painted doors. I cleaned her up and took her back over to play with Casey.

I had started painting again when my husband and David came back in the house. "Do you realize what Tiffany is doing?" he shouted at me. "Of course, she's feeding Casey." She was feeding Casey a handful, and then Tiffany ate a handful!

[THE SHORTER VERSION] *By Kathy Perry*

BIG BUCKS

My son informed me the other day that since he'll be driving this year he's going to need "big bucks." Just the other day he asked me for money—I said, "Sure sweetheart, you can have all the money I have." His eyes lit up as he hurried to get my purse before I changed my mind. "Very funny," he shouted as he pulled the two dollars out of my purse. "Where's the rest of it?" he inquired. "I spent it" I shouted. "I sent the servants their salary, and the money for groceries for our house in Marthas Vineyard." I sent the crew of our yacht their salary, they need to get the ship ready for a bash we're throwing next week.

He looked at me like I was brain dead. "Very funny."

I'd like to introduce you to a new word. It's called a job. You will have your own paycheck to "blow" on stupid things like gas, car payments, insurance and food. You'll have your own money to spend on "women."

And you know what?" I smiled "I can't wait til I look in your billfold and say-where did all your money go?"

[THE SHORTER VERSION] By Kathy Perry

MOM SAYS I CAN

As my husband sat on the rowing machine, sweating to death, I sat in the room with him telling him how sad I felt. "I've been working out for about 10 months now," I began. "You would think after all this time I would start to lose weight. On the days I don't do the 20-minute workout, I work out on the rowing machine." My husband never stopped. He continued rowing and occasionally nodded his head to let me know he was still listening to me.
"You would think after all this time I would be able to wear a smaller size; but no, not me. I've gone up two! You said muscle weighs more than fat and that I would gain at first. I had occasion to see myself in a full-length mirror the other day. I look like a fat Popeye! My goal was Olive Oyl."
I kept talking for about ten more minutes. When I looked over at my husband, he wasn't rowing he was smiling.
"What did I say that's so funny?" "Nothing, really. He wiped his face with the towel and walked over to where I was sitting. "I think you need to watch your diet." In my defense I began, "You know I drink diet pop and mineral water and eat lots of salad and even rice cakes." He smiled again. "I know you eat rice cakes. But you can't eat rice cakes with marshmallow cream on them and then wash it down with a big glass of chocolate milk."
"Well, my Mom says I can!"

[THE SHORTER VERSION] *By Kathy Perry*

AMY'S COOKING

Since the kids have been "visiting" this summer, I've been having trouble cooking. The first night they were all gone I cooked spaghetti. My husband asked me if we were having company. I told him no and we ate spaghetti for the next 14 days. We decided to eat out the next two nights. I stopped and got chicken one night. A few nights when it was so hot we decided to swim first and eat later. One night I came home from work and took a nap. I don't remember eating at all that night. Amy called and said she was homesick, so I picked her up. Everything in the fridge is for one or two people. So far, the idea of eating rice cakes hasn't thrilled her. She hates my diet pop and she said she's tired of salad. When I come home from work she has lots of ideas about what we should do for the evening, and none of those ideas has to do with a nap. I guess I have to go to the store and buy the "good stuff" as Amy puts it. When I told my husband what we were having for dinner, he said he forgot about a meeting he had and we shouldn't wait dinner for him. He would stop later for a sandwich. I said, "It's too bad you won't be home for dinner tonight because Amy was planning to cook spaghetti."

[THE SHORTER VERSION] *By Kathy Perry*

WHIRLWIND WEEK

This has been an unusual week to say the least. I told my husband that on a one to ten scale this week was about a two. One being the worst. Everyone has been all mixed up. I have a dog who thinks she's a cat. She doesn't meow or anything, but she eats all the cat food. I have a cat who likes to sit in the dog's dish and play with the Kibbles 'n' Bits. Sometimes she likes to eat a few pieces of dog food. It's probably just to get even with the dog for eating all her food. I have children who think my ancestors were the Rockefellers. They think I have somehow managed to tap into Fort Knox. When I tell them I don't have any more money, they say use your credit card or write a check. I just found out my husband doesn't know how to spell my first name.

My daughter whom I had just covered with calamine lotion, tried to convince me that the little girl she had been sharing a sleeping bag with, who had poison ivy, that it wasn't contagious. The most confused of all is my neighbor. When I got home from work the other night, she called to see if we had any wind damage at our house.

"No," I told her, "but you know what, Deb, it was the craziest thing. As I was driving home I saw about 15 or 20 little whirlwinds in front of my car. By the time I got up to them they had joined forces and were one big whirlwind. I thought it looked like a tornado, but kept driving through it. How about your house?"

"Well," she started, "you remember that chicken coop out back?"

"Yeah, I remember."

"Now it's in my living room."

[THE SHORTER VERSION] By Kathy Perry

MISSION IMPOSSIBLE

The other day I realized there are several things in my life I have no control over. I decided they are things I should label "impossible missions" and accept my fate. One of the things I have no control over is the fact that my children are separate beings. They ignore dirty glasses on the coffee table, wet towels on the bathroom floor or on their bedspread. When all the glasses are dirty, they don't wash them, they either get out the good glasses, or they use paper cups. When they have dirty laundry, they wash exactly what it is they want to wear the next day. Even if there are 20 pairs of jeans in the hamper, they only wash one pair of jeans, one shirt, and maybe underwear. And, of course, that's all they dry.

The other "mission" is trying to get them to eat. Well, I shouldn't say "eat" because they live to eat. It's what they eat I object to. Nachos in cheese sauce, tacos, Quarter Pounders with cheese. I know they eat that stuff because I have recognized the wrappers in their cars. I've tried to get them to sit in the dining room with the rest of us, but they always say, "I'll grab something later, Mom."

I guess I survived. My mother used to tell me not to eat so much chocolate. And not to drink so much pop. I didn't listen to her either. I used to drink pop for breakfast. In fact, I still drink pop on Saturday morning along with a bag of pretzels. That's probably my favorite summertime breakfast.

It's no wonder my children are such health food nuts. They had a great teacher.

[THE SHORTER VERSION] *By Kathy Perry*

SHE DRIVES A CAB

My husband and I were invited to a party over the weekend, and it was far enough away from home that we decided we would stay all night. It's not often we stay anywhere all night because of all the preparations that must be made. I have to find temporary homes for my children and I have to make sure someone will check on my animals. Karen and Nick were the ideal host and hostess, and I was able to meet lots of people. I'm never surprised when the conversation turns back to children. God made all children equal. When he made teenagers, he used a special mold. Teenagers everywhere know more than their mom and dad. Dad is not excluded here. Dads are dumb too, until the kid reaches 20, then Dad is the smartest person in the world.

As I mingled with the groups, I listened to different mothers discuss their children's problems. One of the problems was a baby who stayed up all night wanting to be fed. Another child fought with siblings. And one whole room was for parents of teenagers. The group in the kitchen was a lively bunch. Most of them were either single or childless. Those were the people who were talking about nice vacations, the designer clothes, the expensive cars. And they seemed to laugh a lot. My husband kept finding me and I would point him in the direction of the "football" area. He kept coming back. While he was sitting with me he would usually bring up the fact that I'm a writer. And the people would start to ask me questions. I would just nod my head and change the subject. But not my husband. He had to go into great detail about my columns.

"I'm always afraid to say the wrong thing in front of her," he started. "She gets this weird look on her face and then runs upstairs to her office."

One lady looked at him and said, "You mean writers actually write about people they know?"

THE SHORTER VERSION
By Kathy Perry

"Of course, "he shouted. "And her humor is usually directed at me."

I looked at my husband as the fourth group of people started to shy away from me.

"Do you think you could do me a favor," I glared at him. "Could you just tell people I drive a cab?"

[THE SHORTER VERSION] *By Kathy Perry*

IT FITS

I've decided it's time to diet, when I'm folding laundry and my son can tell from across the room which jeans are mine.

The only thing that's comfortable is an elastic waistband. I used to be able to stand next to my mother to feel thin, but now we can wear each others clothes. At least I don't have to answer stupid questions any more about how I stay so thin. Those days are gone forever.

My husband keeps reminding me if I didn't eat chocolate chip cookies, strawberry pie, Klondike bars and bags of peanut M&M's, I'd be able to lose weight. I told him I wouldn't eat all that stuff if I didn't like it. Besides chocolate is one of the basic food groups, isn't it?

He tells me there's no hope, that I should just buy new clothes.

Last week while I was exercising, my son yelled at my husband that they had to put more braces under the floor, as they both ran to the basement laughing hysterically. I'm sick of rice cakes and salad. I'm tired of having my husband stand on my stomach just to get my jeans zipped.

I've decided I'm going to organize a club. It's for fat people only. We are going to have potluck dinners and never mention DIET.

I think the high point of my week was when I stopped at Porter's for dinner the other night. We decided to go to the fair at the last minute and I didn't have a jacket.

Don't ever let it be said that Mike Porter won't give you the shirt off his back-it wasn't his shirt but his jacket---and it fit!

[THE SHORTER VERSION] *By Kathy Perry*

ONE MORE TIME

This week two different moms came to see me. One of them was upset about her young children, the other mom was upset about her teenagers. I remember my grandmother used to tell me "when they are young, they step on your toes and as they get older they step on your heart." The mother of the young children was frazzled because her children were all sick. One with an ear infection, another with bronchitis and another with the flu. Her husband had just started a new job and of course, the first week he was not home to help her very much. By the time she came home from work, picked up the kids from the sitters, and tried to take care of the kid's needs, she was a wreck. She was physically and emotionally exhausted.

My other friend was exhausted too. Because after 18 years of caring and guidance and loving she learned her daughter is using drugs. The day she came to see me she didn't know where her daughter was. She didn't even know what state she was in. All my friend could do was cry, She kept telling me she felt like a failure as a mom. She said "we always went to church, we went to movies and ball games together. I thought we were doing all the 'right' things."

None of us want our kids to "turn out bad", anymore than we want them to be sick when they are little. Almost every time I pick up the paper I read about another alcohol or drug related accident involving teenagers. I was appalled to learn that the second killer of our teenagers is suicide, second to drugs or alcohol.

I don't know what the answer is, or when the problem will be resolved.

I think every parent I know prays that their child won't be the next victim of drugs, alcohol or suicide, or the next statistic. I pray for that too.

[THE SHORTER VERSION] *By Kathy Perry*

MY DAD CAN DO IT

I remember when I was little I used to think my dad could fix anything. He was my hero. If I had a broken toy, my dad could fix it. If mom's washer was broken, dad could fix that too.

I got a little older; he was still pretty smart, but not as smart as he had been.

By the time I was a teenager, he didn't know much about anything. However, even though I didn't really need him, I still asked him to fix the flat tire on my bike. When I started driving a car, it wasn't dad I called, but my mom because I knew dad would yell. He was still the one who came to my rescue. He yelled a lot because I had been driving too fast and the car over heated. He always reminded me of that fact before I borrowed his car. I thought he just liked to yell at me.

It was a strange process, because the older and wiser I got, the older and wiser he got too.

When I started dating my husband, I had to be careful, because I always told my husband my dad could do anything. Over the years, my husband feels the same way about my dad.

A few days ago, we were installing a ceiling fan. Several of the screws had been painted on the motor and we couldn't remove them. We took the fan down and took it to my dad and in just a matter of minutes, he had loosened that screw. I smiled at my mom and gave her a hug. "You're the smartest lady I know, Mom."

She just looked at me.

"You picked Dad."

[THE SHORTER VERSION] *By Kathy Perry*

FRIDAY THE 13TH

It's time for me to plan another vacation. I think it will be week after next, because Amy has decided she wants to have a slumber party for her birthday this year, instead of a small family gathering. She said that would be boring, because all she would be able to do would be open presents and eat cake and ice cream.

I said, "Amy, I will cook all your favorites and we will sing to you."

She looked at me unsympathetically, "Mom, you can still cook my favorites. How about if we start out with tacos?"

I asked her if she would like to play a few games, like pin the tail on the donkey. She looked at me like I was brain dead.

"Mom, I'm not a little girl any more. We want to rent a few movies. We can watch movies while you go pick up pizzas."

I told her I would be glad to pick up a few movies.

"What would you like, Winnie the Pooh or Willy Wonka and the Chocolate Factory?"

She put her hand on her hip and looked at me like I just told her she had to kiss her brother.

"Mom," she shouted, "we want Fright Night and Friday the 13th."

[THE SHORTER VERSION]   *By Kathy Perry*

JUST LIKE A BOY

When I was a little girl I remember my grandmother used to tell me not to laugh at anyone "less fortunate" than we were.
I had no idea what she meant by "less fortunate."
At any rate, I learned at an early age not to laugh at someone else's mistake.
Several months ago a friend stopped by my desk on a Monday morning.
I looked up from my paperwork and noticed she had gotten another perm.
"Didn't you just have your hair permed a few weeks ago?"
"Yes," she shouted at me, "and don't say a word about it! I know if you were in my situation you would have done the same thing."
I was almost afraid to ask her what she was talking about.
"Not to worry, she continued. "My daughter begged me for a month to have her hair permed, so I called and made an appointment for her several weeks ago. Well, on Friday night she decided she didn't want a perm, and since I didn't want to make my hairdresser upset, I got the perm."
By then I was biting my lip to keep from laughing.
My own daughter wanted a perm too, about a month ago. I didn't think it was a good idea, but I let her do it. After several weeks of arguing with her about combing the tangles out of her permed hair, I decided she should get it cut. She looked up at me through tear-filled eyes.
"Mom, I wanted long hair. Now, my hair will be shorter than yours." I smiled at her. "Would it make you feel better if I got a haircut, too?"
"Yes, " she said.
Since my hair was short to start with, by the time the hair dresser was finished…Well, just let me say that when I came home my son said. "From the back, Mom, you look just like a boy"!

[THE SHORTER VERSION] *By Kathy Perry*

SOUNDS GOOD TO ME

Why is it nobody ever puts anything away at my house. If they get the milk out, they leave it on the counter in the kitchen. If they need a glass or a cup, they leave the cupboard open. A peanut butter sandwich? Sure, the bread is still on the counter, the peanut butter is there beside the open bread wrapper. After all these years they have learned to put the lid back on the peanut butter jar. I can follow my kids through the house. Food, clothes, towels, empty glasses on the coffee table. When they do put the milk away there is only about a tablespoon left. When they are old enough to leave home the only thing they take is your curling iron or hair dryer. They never remember their dog or cat that they promised to "take with them everywhere they went". When you visit, they ask you to please turn you glass upside down in the sink, after you rinse it of course. If you dry your hands in the kitchen, would you mind using a paper towel because now she must go to the laundromat. And how about coming over for dinner mom? As I'm walking out the door on my way to her house, the phone is ringing.

"Mom, I know I invited you over for dinner, but would you mind picking up a pizza and bringing it over, I'm pretty tired."

[THE SHORTER VERSION] By Kathy Perry

NO SQUIRREL FOR DAD

When I was a little girl I used to beg my dad to take me with him squirrel hunting. I don't really think I wanted to hunt, I just wanted to be with my dad.

To this day, my father loves to tell anyone who will listen about our one and only experience.

I was only eight or nine years old and it's one of my fondest memories. We walked to get all the way back to the woods, talking all the way. After we got to the edge of the woods, he told me we'd have to be quiet. I remember how hard that was for me, even then, I had so many things I wanted to tell my dad and of course I wanted to help him find a squirrel, but I didn't really want him to shoot one of those cute little creatures. He decided I should sit by a tree and wait for him. He threatened me not to move a hair. So I waited patiently for him to return.

My dad remembers that morning entirely differently. He remembers I would not shut up from the time we left the house until the time we reached the woods. When we reached the woods, I stepped on sticks all the while talking about how I hoped we would see a little squirrel. He decided to sit me somewhere by myself so I would stop talking. He said I did stop talking but grew bored and started breaking twigs. Deciding he wouldn't give up he would try one more time to get me to be quiet. So he said, "Now, let's just sit here and be real quiet until we see a squirrel."

I wanted him to be proud of me and I knew I could do it—that is until I saw a squirrel. I jumped to my feet and shouted, "There it is, Dad!"

And then we were on our way home.

[THE SHORTER VERSION] *By Kathy Perry*

LIFESTYLES OF THE POOR & UNKNOWN

I WATCHED A SHOW THE OTHER DAY, "lifestyles of the Rich and Famous," I wish they would produce a show I could identify with, like "Lifestyles of the Poor and Unknown."
One of my main problems is which coast to buy my next house on, or how to staff it for the three weeks I'm there. Get real!
I could relate to women rushing through the grocery store with coupons in hand sorting out the "bargains."
Or pushing each other out of the way at a "midnight madness" sale.
Maybe a tour through the poor and unknown's house. Mom is walking through the door at 5:45 p.m. with a bag of groceries in one arm and a gallon of milk in the other hand. The kids are in front of the TV and the remains of their after-school snacks are sitting on the coffee table. All the cupboard doors are open in this "poor" person's kitchen. The half-full gallon of milk is sitting on the counter.
As the TV camera follows this weary mom down the hall to the master bedroom, she tries to pull her son's bedroom door closed, but there are clothes falling into the hall. His sister's room, which is the next room, looks like it blew up, things hanging from the ceiling and the lamp shades.
Mom isn't on her way to the master suite to relax in a sauna while the live-in cook prepares dinner; no, she's changing her clothes while her children are following closely behind her shoving each other into the wall screaming, "What's for dinner?" But before mom can cook, she has to shove dirty clothes out of the way. I'm not saying this is the lifestyle I prefer—the poor and unknown, it' just one I can identify with.

[THE SHORTER VERSION] By Kathy Perry

MY MOUNTAIN MAN

Living with "The Mountain Man" sure has changed my life.
I never know from one day to the next if it's safe to step from my car. There are box traps, an axe with a broken handle and a lot of "junk" dropped on the floor because he "needed" the can the trash was in. And over head he has the fur from the "creatures" he caught, hanging to dry in my garage.
His Carharts are drying over a chair in the dining room. His tennis shoes are on the first step of the basement stairs, so that when I'm rushing down those stairs with a basket full of dirty laundry I almost break my neck. I haven't been able to understand why he can go outside during rain, sleet or hail to check his traps, but it's too cold, wet or dark to burn the trash.
My favorite is when my little dog goes outside, he always finds the remains of the Mountain man's creatures and he loves to roll on it or bring it in the house. Whenever I ask Mountain Man about it he always tells me he buried it.
He told me just the other day how much money he's making this year, told me how he planned to put "most" of it in the bank. I said "That's great, now you can start paying for your own lunch."
The next morning as he was leaving for school he shouted, "Mom can I take some money from your purse for lunch?"
"I thought you had your own money now."
"I do, Mom, but I hate to break a $20."

[THE SHORTER VERSION] *By Kathy Perry*

HE'S A CHEF

During the past few years my husband has been trying to learn to cook. I told him before we were married I've always admired a man who could cook. I said "I've got a real good cookbook-even you could learn to cook."
He just wrinkled his nose at me.
"I could cook," he stated, "but no one could eat it."
Amy and I lived through Oatmeal and Cream of Wheat that was so salty we could have spread it on the icy walk. He prepared Jello that was layered rock.
He made popcorn one night and didn't get the lid on right-so popcorn shot all over the kitchen. During the summer he attempted hamburgers and hot dogs on the grill. By the end of summer he graduated to chicken. One night black smoke filled the kitchen. Amy met me at the door and said in a calm voice, "Don't worry Mom. Dad's just cooking dinner." It was garlic bread he had forgotten about. Amy said the smoke reminded him. In the fall he decided he wanted to try something a little more "advanced," so I bought several frozen dinner entrees like turkey and roast beef. He was so proud the first night when I came home we had turkey, mashed potatoes, corn and dinner rolls. I told him we could open a "turkey" restaurant. During the next few weeks we had turkey fourteen times. So I thought-this guy is getting pretty good-but I don't think I can eat any more turkey-so I brought home a pot roast and held it up proudly. "Look what I bought for you."
He was sitting in the living room, "What is it?"
"It's a pot roast," I shouted with joy.
"Well, what do I do with it?" he questioned.
"My first clue would be to heat it."

[THE SHORTER VERSION] *By Kathy Perry*

HE BURST MY BUBBLE

Last week I traded my sweat suit for a paint brush. I was so excited a few weeks ago while I was browsing around the Hobby Horse, I spotted a painting I loved. I was impressed with the colors and how she had mixed the depth. I had been searching for over two years for another art instructor. Ever since Audrey died I had not found anyone I was impressed with until last week.

I got out all my old painting supplies, checked and cleaned my brushes. My family got sick of hearing me talk about "Iris."

But I didn't let them dampen my spirits.

I was so excited during the class. I was even more impressed with Iris in person. She's lively, enthusiastic, creative, positive and a fireball with an infectious laugh. We told her we would take any art class she would teach. I was still so excited all the way home. I couldn't wait to show my family what Iris had helped me create on the canvas. My husband just smiled, patted me on the back and mumbled something about the colors. I was still bubbling over with excitement until I turned to my son.

"Look, honey, look what I painted, where do you think I should hang it?"

Without skipping a beat my six foot tall son put his arm around my shoulder and said, "I think this painting would look great on your side of the garage, Mom."

[THE SHORTER VERSION]   By Kathy Perry

TWAS THE NIGHT BEFORE CHRISTMAS

"T'was the night before Christmas and all through the house…..." That is one of my fondest childhood memories.
Of course no night is calm at my house.
As we approach Christmas, I find myself wishing for snow. I want to have a snowball fight with my son or make a snowman with my little girl or bake cookies with my big girl. The older I become, the more I realize how important my family and friends are. I need my family and friends close by. It is impossible for me to call or even write a note to all of you, who over the years have sent me a note, or called me on the phone or even stopped me on the street to tell me you liked (or didn't like) my article. To you, my faithful followers, I want to say thank you for your support and encouragement. My special wish for everyone this season would be to continue the feeling of love and hope and compassion for those around you today, tomorrow and every day next year.
We have the privilege of loving everyone, but we never know how long we'll get to love them.
My family's wish is for a Merry Christmas to all. May God Bless each and everyone of you.
So hug each other-from me- "Merry Christmas to all---and to all a good night"……

THE SHORTER VERSION
By Kathy Perry

BRAIN DEAD

I'm not sure how much "dumber" I have to get before my kids realize I haven't been declared "brain dead."

For years I have been doing laundry without an instruction booklet. But now all of a sudden my daughter realizes I can't be trusted to do her laundry.

I've had a drivers license for a long time---according to them the first car I drove was a Model T Ford-but they don't like the way I drive their cars.

They would rather eat out than have "Mom's home cooking." My roast beef gets caught in their teeth. They don't like my mashed potatoes because they "take too long." They prefer macaroni and cheese from a box. They don't like the way I talk. To be gay means happy.

I don't understand their problems because "you just don't understand."

My clothes and shoes are from the "Roaring 20's"

My hair and make-up are "funky."

They don't like the way I spend my money, because there's never enough for them. The would prefer I paid the bills after they spend what they want.

The other day my son wanted $50 for something. When I told him I didn't have any money he said, "You just got paid, what did you do with all your money?" I said "I gave half of it to Amy and we went to the mall to see which one of us could buy clothes and spend it the fastest!"

I think there's still hope, because I turned to Amy and said, "You know Amy, someday you'll treat me just like your sister does."

She quietly came to my rescue, "Yeah, Mom, but I'm not gonna' call you names like my brother."

[THE SHORTER VERSION] *By Kathy Perry*

BE NICE TO MOM

My girlfriend Sharon has been staying with her mother since her mother's recent knee surgery. Sharon has two teenaged boys and a husband in addition to a full-time job. She is such an optimistic person and I love her to pieces.

We have so much in common, mainly "teenagers." So many times she's related stories about how the "boys" don't appreciate her, how they never listen to her advice (or even ask for it) and how they only speak to her in a normal tone when they want money or the car.

I've always admired her courage and hoped I could be as levelheaded as she.

Last week I failed miserably. I only had a few hours one day to do several loads of laundry, cook and clean the house before I had to go back to the nursing home to visit my friend.

When I came home my son was stretched out on the sofa in front of the TV. When he heard me, he tried to act like he was asleep. I asked him to take out the trash, he was too tired. When I asked him to fill the wood box he couldn't find his shoes. I asked him to shake the throw rugs and he had already found his shoes but taken them off again.

He finally admitted he wanted me to take him and a friend to a movie that night. I told him sure, but that I would only take him one way because that's the way he did everything for me. He said that was fine because his friend's mother had agreed to drive them "one way too."

I felt like he had really gotten away with being selfish all day. But I got him.

He came back in the house after getting water for the dog.

"How soon will dinner be ready Mom? It sure smells good. What is it?" he shouted.

To which I replied "it will be ready before you and Todd leave for the movie, and it's your favorite---pig snout!"

[THE SHORTER VERSION] *By Kathy Perry*

ROCK HIM GENTLY

Anyone who knows me, knows how I feel about my little dog KoKo. In fact sometime I am offended if people refer to him as a "dog." He looks at me with those little brown eyes and my heart melts. He never leaves my side. If I'm in the kitchen cooking, he sleeps on the rug by the sink. If I'm watching TV, he snuggles beside me on the sofa. If I'm in the basement folding clothes or doing laundry, he barks until I bring him with me or I come back upstairs. When I take my keys out of my purse, he waits at the door, because he loves to ride in the car so he can smear my windows with his little nose. If I'm at my desk working on a manuscript, he is always at my feet. He's never happy when I'm in the bathroom unless the door is open so he can come and go at will.

My son loves to play a game with him. It's called tease KoKo. My son will come into the room and hit me on the arm or hand or leg so that KoKo will go crazy and bite at him. KoKo hates anyone who touches me. When Amy tries to sit next to me for a hug or kiss, KoKo very rudely squeezes between us, then sticks his nose up in the air, so we can "kiss" him on the "cheek" too.

My husband says I have ruined the dog. I say I have made him precious. My husband says he is spoiled and a wimp. I say he is tough and courageous.

Last week one day my husband got stuck with KoKo. I was only gone for a few hours, but my husband said KoKo cried the whole time I was gone.

"That dumb dog ran from one window to the other waiting for your car to pull in the driveway. You've ruined the dog," he said.

"Of course I haven't ruined him," I said. "You just don't know how to take care of him. All he wanted you to do was pick him up and rock him."

[THE SHORTER VERSION]   *By Kathy Perry*

AMY'S BIG DAY

I don't think Amy has ever been as happy as she was last Tuesday.
Not only was it the "Opening Night" of "Get Hoppin" but she was also selected as student of the month.
I was so proud of her and all her little friends. They were so good they were requested to give four other performances.
Amy called all her friends and relatives to invite them to her performance. From the looks of the auditorium that night all the other kids did the same thing. She has been reminding me since Christmas vacation about her play. In all the years I've sat through PTO meetings and grade school plays I've never gone to one where the cast received a standing ovation.
When I picked Amy up from Brownies that night she was so excited her eyes talked. I didn't have to wait long to find out why she was so excited.
"Mom, guess what, today Miss Ferrington asked me to go to Miss Roarty's office. When I got to her office she asked me to sit down and take off my jacket. I thought I was in BIG trouble. Then she said she wanted to take my picture.
I think she could tell I was mixed up. Then guess what Mom, she explodes, "I'm Student of the Month.!"

[THE SHORTER VERSION] By Kathy Perry

A MILLIONAIRE

I didn't have to work the other day, so I slept in, until 8:30 anyway. I walked to the kitchen, scratching my head, yawning, looking for the teapot. All I wanted to do was have a cup of tea and read the paper. You know, when you have the day off it's nice to be able to do what you want to do.

I became so depressed when I actually looked at my reflection in the full-length mirror. The face looked familiar, but the hair and body must be a mistake. Everything from below my neck had gone south. My hair was gray and my nail polish chipped. I picked up the phone and called my hairdresser.

"I just made the mistake of looking at myself in the mirror."

She laughed, "It can't be that bad. Why don't you come on in. You can lie in the tanning bed. Kim can do your nails, and I'll do something to your hair."

Sounded easy enough.

I remembered when my son was younger I used to say "it took me 20 minutes to get this beautiful." To which he always replied, "Mom, I think you better take another 20 minutes."

The older I get, the longer it takes. You have to put on all this stuff to conceal age spots and warts and moles on your face. You have to "cover" the gray. And you have to put something on those brown spots on your hands, the ones you always asked your grandmother what they were.

After I spent a couple hours there, I started to feel a little better. As I stood to leave I happened to look in her mirror. "You know Bonnie, if you could get rid of this (pointing to my behind) in just an hour you would be a millionaire."

[THE SHORTER VERSION] — *By Kathy Perry*

ABOUT TWO YEARS AGO

I read a survey the other day about motherhood. I always wondered where they find the people for those surveys.

Of the women they surveyed 70 percent of them said they wouldn't be mothers again. This survey also discovered that adolescence was the least liked stage. I'm sure it didn't take an Einstein to figure that one out. The two people doing the study concluded that by raising our children to be independent we create obnoxious children who talk back. Somehow it wasn't really all that comforting knowing that I'm not the only mother whose teenagers like her for her food, money and car.

The survey went on to say that today's mother is doing more and getting less help from her husband.

The other day one of my friends was complaining about her teenagers.

She said "you know, my husband never pays any attention to our daughter any more. They used to be so close." She continued, "for the last two years she has been so mean to me, it's like she hates me. She yells at me, calls me at work to ask for money, and always wants my car."

"The other night the three of us sat down to a nice, quiet dinner and of course she exploded and ruined my evening."

She continued. "Listen to this, my husband looked at me and said, "When did she get so lippy?"

[THE SHORTER VERSION] *By Kathy Perry*

ON MY OWN

It is a wonderful feeling, knowing your children have finally moved out and are able to make it on their own. And I'm still lucid enough to remember their names.

After several weeks of packing boxes and trying to buy paper towels, toilet paper, and a few other things to help out, I think we finally got the last box and bag out of her room. It looks so different now. It's been years since I've seen the floor. I had forgotten what color the carpet was. I didn't remember how big the room was. She always had clothes draped over chairs, light fixtures, and dressers, so I was surprised when she carried so much furniture out of there. I tried to convert her room into an office for me, so I wouldn't feel sad every time I looked in her room and she wasn't there.

I moved my typewriter and a few plants in there and started feeling good about my new "space"; the phone rang. It was my daughter inviting me over for dinner. My joy was short-lived however, as I pulled in the driveway I recognized the lawn mower she was using.

Hope you don't mind, Mom." Her brother said it was okay if she borrowed it. Somehow that didn't surprise me.

We went in the house and I recognized a few clothes baskets full of bath towels. I gave her a few small kitchen appliances, like a mixer and wooden spoons.

"This is nice. Now you can have a pet."

"Heavens no Mother! I don't want all that mess with a new puppy."

I'm counting on my fingers the puppies she brought home over the years.

"By the way Mom, we'll bring your mower back this weekend."

Great, I'm thinking to myself, she's probably going to offer to cut our grass for Father's Day. What a nice gesture.

THE SHORTER VERSION — By Kathy Perry

She continued, "I thought I would drop off the mower and pick up your grill. I'd like to have a few friends over to celebrate making it on my own."

[THE SHORTER VERSION] *By Kathy Perry*

GIRLS HAVE TO DO EVERYTHING

I was sitting in the dining room the other day drinking iced tea, trying to cool off after mowing the lawn. I was reading the paper when I felt a little hand tap me on the shoulder.

"Can we talk, Mom?"

"Sure, Amy, what would you like to talk about?"

She pulled up a chair, took a sip of my iced tea, then sat back and crossed her arms. She looked very pensive for a moment.

"You know Mom, I was just thinking the other day about how life is really not fair."

"I know Amy, it sure seems like that sometimes."

She looked out the dining room window, then she said, "Sometimes it's not fair Mom because you get to do all the fun stuff and you make me do all the work, and I'm just a little kid."

I nodded my head.

"Like the other day when you were painting the ceiling and I asked you if I could help. You said maybe later. (I meant in three or four years), but all I got to do was find the roller pan and move the ladder a few times. Then a few days later you got to put wall paper on the walls and I asked you if I could help and you said sure I need the scissors. Well, I wanted to stick the paper in the water and then put it on the wall too.

"And then yesterday I wanted to cut the grass. You said "Why don't you pull the weeds in the flower bed." Well, they're your flowers, Mom. And one more thing, I'm tired of taking out the trash. I could get burned."

She sat there a little while longer. I was thinking of things in my defense. She took another drink of my iced tea, in fact she drank the rest of it.

"Well, I'm really glad you were born a girl. Why does that make you unhappy?"

"If you would just think about it Mom, it would make you unhappy too. We have to clean the house, go to the grocery

[THE SHORTER VERSION] *By Kathy Perry*

store, cook, wash the dishes and the laundry. All my Dad and my brother do is come home, read the paper, watch TV then go to bed. Girls have to do everything."

[THE SHORTER VERSION] By Kathy Perry

MOTHER DEAREST

Several years ago someone asked me if I was like my mother. "Heavens no!" I replied. Let me tell you about my mother. She's a saver and a shopper. She saves everything. She reuses bread wrappers, she saves the twist ties. She has a closet for those plastic margarine tubs. She washes and reuses plastic forks. When she sees "sale" she's in the car. "Two for one," don't get in her way.

I suppose over the years I have started to think a little like my mother. When there's a sale now, we call each other to brag about who found the better bargain. She saves magazines and newspapers, and has drawers full of aluminum foil. She saves the trays the little frozen dinners come in. And she has grocery sacks full of those little pot pie tins.

"Mom why do you have all this stuff?"

"You never know when some of that stuff might come in handy."

Ah, yes, that's my mother!

The other day my daughter came over, the one who has her own apartment now, and she was helping me put groceries away. First she opened one drawer, then another and finally another. She turned around to look at me with a slight smile on her lips.

"Mom, what is all this junk you've collected? Why do you need all those bread wrappers, or those twist ties, or all that aluminum foil? I can't believe it, you're just like grandma."

To which I replied, " You never know when some of that stuff might come in handy."

[THE SHORTER VERSION] *By Kathy Perry*

NO TV

My girlfriend called the other day just to see how things were going for me. "Just the usual," I started to say. "How are things with you?"
I had a feeling we were going to be on the phone for a long time when I heard her take a deep breath.
"Well, the doctor removed the stitches from my knee last week."
I started telling her about feeling like I never have any time to myself. Everyone wants a piece of my time. Between my job, my kids, school and housework, there is never any time left for me. My kids expect me to cancel my plans if they have something they want me to do. But if I ask them for help they act like I just committed an ax murder.
"Well, listen to this," my friend shouted. "You know how helpful my kids have been since my surgery. I had to stay off my leg. Nobody would cook for me. One day my husband threw me a bag of cookies as he left for work. They left me a bowl of water! I finally learned to balance food on a plate while walking on crutches. I even carried a bag of potato chips between my teeth. You get desperate. My daughter came home from school one day and asked me what we were having for dinner. My leg was packed in ice, propped up on the ottoman and she almost tripped over my crutches!"
"But what happened today is even worse,"she continued. "I finally got rid of my crutches and I was able to drive myself to the doctors office. My knee is still filling with fluid so the doctor had to drain it again. I was sitting there holding the nurses hand, trying to keep from crying while the doctor was taking fluid from my knee, when the receptionist came in the room to let me know I had a telephone call. The doctor finished withdrawing the fluid and they both helped me to the outer office to the phone. It was my other daughter. She wanted me to come to her apartment to pick her up and take her to the drug

THE SHORTER VERSION
By Kathy Perry

store because she had a cold sore. She also wanted me to take her uptown to pay her cable TV bill. After we did all those things I drove myself home, hobbled to the living room and sank onto the sofa.

As I sat there thinking about my afternoon, and the wait I had while she was paying her cable bill, I remembered," she doesn't even own a TV."

[THE SHORTER VERSION] *By Kathy Perry*

HAPPY THANKSGIVING

My kids always make fun of me because I tell them my favorite holiday is Thanksgiving. They probably wouldn't make fun of me if I didn't say the same thing about Easter, Memorial Day, the Fourth of July, Labor Day and Christmas. Just like all my favorite seasons, Spring, Summer, Fall and Winter. I really do enjoy Thanksgiving, because it is the one day in the middle of the week when my family always gets together and we talk about anything and everything. We sit and stuff ourselves and lie about the diets we all plan to start later. The older I grow the more thankful I am for my family and friends and the special memories we are making. The other day I was reminiscing about past Thanksgivings. One particular Thanksgiving came to mind. That was the one when I cooked my first turkey. I used to love to wake up on Thanksgiving morning when I was a kid and smell Mom's turkey cooking. I thought Mom stuck it in the oven the night before. I had no idea you didn't have to cook it 12 or 16 hours. Imagine my surprise. I remember how frustrated I was trying to pull the legs out, and how important it was when I broke a nail. I was so proud of myself for finding a recipe for homemade stuffing (that was before Stove Top) that I was sure everyone would make comments about one Thanksgiving to the next. And probably beg me to make it every year. When I started stuffing the still frozen bird, I wasn't able to get more than just a few tablespoons in there, so I just threw the rest of it in the pan around the turkey.

Well, surprise, surprise. Thank God for Mothers. I had called her in a panic that morning anyway, because my gravy was still at the 'dumpling's state. You know, when the lumps in the gravy are the size of grandmothers dumplings. Anyway, Mom came over early and just stood there shaking her head.

"It's a good thing you're smart, honey, because you will never be the next Julia Child. First of all, you have stuffed the wrong

[THE SHORTER VERSION] *By Kathy Perry*

end of the turkey. And I was wondering what you did with the giblets, for the giblet gravy"

As I turned around to grab the lid on the potatoes that were now boiling over, I noticed my mother pulling something out of the turkey.

"Here they are," she shouted, as if she had just caught a ten pound cat fish."

I had cooked the little bag of giblets inside the turkey.

Well, nobody told me.

[THE SHORTER VERSION] *By Kathy Perry*

HELLO CHICAGO

Chicago will never be the same. When Barb, Sharon, Libby and I decided to go Christmas shopping, I thought they meant Columbus.

When they first told me their plan they said, "Lets take Amtrak." That sounded like fun---until later. They didn't bother to tell me that we had to leave from Crestline at 3 a.m. "Oh, we'll pick you up at 2 a.m." No problem- I can sleep on the train-fat chance.

The train stopped so many times between here and Chicago, and each time they stopped they turned all the lights on to welcome the next group of people. When we arrived in Chicago, of course our room wasn't ready, so I couldn't even brush my teeth for two hours.

The next experience was trying to hail a cab. We were trying to get their attention from inside the hotel because it was so cold and windy outside. We tried to walk the "magnificent mile" until we realized that it was seven miles long.

We shopped at Bonwit Teller, Saks and I Magnin. We saw Barry Manilow in concert. We ate dinner at midnight at the Hard Rock Café and rode in a cab through the streets of Chicago at 2 a.m. trying to take pictures of all the Christmas lights. "One" of us got to sleep on a roll-away bed even though we all had to pay full price.

We visited the Water Tower and the Sears Building, and we ate in the Artists Snack Shop. We had dessert and a hundred different flavors of coffee before we ran to catch the bus back to the train station.

The only thing we did not do during our 30 hour "get away" was sleep.

We've decided to "save" up for our trip next year. Not money- "SLEEP."

[THE SHORTER VERSION] *By Kathy Perry*

MILITARY LIFE

My son thinks he wants to join the Army or the Navy. He's not aware that he won't be allowed to sleep in on Saturday. He says he's tired of me nagging him about taking out the trash or picking up his clothes. As he walks through the house you can tell where he's been. His shoes or boots and socks are usually in the family room. His coat is on a dining room chair. And he normally leaves a gun part or a knife on the kitchen counter, right beside the peanut butter jar. His eating habits are strange too. It's not strange for him to eat a box of cereal, or a box of Pop Tarts in one day. He usually sits in front of the TV with a gallon of milk and a box of cereal and a large mixing bowl. His idea of a rough day is not shooting a deer, or catching a 50 pound fish. When he comes home from work he likes to take a nap while I'm cooking dinner, and if he falls asleep he doesn't want us to turn off the TV because it will wake him. He thinks military life would be a lot easier than home. All he needs me to do is write down most of my recipes, just in case he doesn't like whatever they cook for him.

[THE SHORTER VERSION] *By Kathy Perry*

WHERE'S MY MOM

A friend of mine decided to "let" her son drive her car to college, because it was newer than his, and she was afraid his might not make it to Colorado. She had been fighting with him for months about going all the way to Colorado. But despite all her arguments he decided to "make it on his own."

She gave him enough money to stay four nights on the road. What she didn't count on was the engine of the car blowing up half-way there. Not only that, he did not have the thousand dollars to pay the repair and tow charges. The reason he called was to let her know he was putting it on her Visa. He added that he would appreciate her sending more money because now her Visa was maxed and he only had money for two more nights. He said he was starving, cold and tired.

For the next three days my poor friend worried about her son, wondering how soon he would reach his destination. She reminded him to call as soon as he arrived, because she was worried. He yelled at her that it wasn't necessary for her to worry because "now he was on his own."

A week later he called home again. She said, "For the first time in my life I'm glad there are so many miles between us---the kid is dangerous. This time when he called it started out like this"

"I decided to go skiing Mom, something I've always wanted to try. The first day I was out I sorta skied off the side of a mountain, and nobody saved me!"

Printed in the United States
92980LV00002B/208-306/A